Beloved

Discovering Your True Identity in Christ

Demi Thompson

To Ernest, Sydney, and Kyle—
for your enduring love and support.

And to the women who labored with me on the threshing floor,
as well as to every other person God has sent my way to say,
"You can make it through this season of life."

I love you with an everlasting love.

CONTENTS

Who You Really Are

Therefore the LORD will wait, that He may be gracious to you; and therefore He will be exalted, that He may have mercy on you...

—Isaiah 30:18a *(NHE)*

You may be looking at this page and wondering why you need to read a book about discovering your identity in Christ. Perhaps you don't even know what an identity in Christ means yet.

Maybe someone recommended this book to you, or maybe something about the cover caught your eye as you wandered the aisle of a bookstore. Whatever the reason that led you to flip to this page, I want you to know God loves you so much and He is actively pursuing a deep and lasting relationship with you. And He's willing to go wherever He needs to in order to meet with you. Even if that means sitting down next to you somewhere in a gutter when you feel like hiding in shame.

Jesus did the same thing when he took a detour on His

way to a place called Galilee when He walked the earth two thousand years ago. While He traveled, He deliberately chose to go *through* a place called Samaria—a land and people shunned by the Jewish people—rather than *around* it. You can read the account for yourself in John 4:1–42, but I'll sum it up for you here. I promise, there's a point to all this!

When Jesus came to the city, He saw a shunned woman drawing water from the well during the heat of the day—a time when no one else who would ridicule or avoid her. Jesus sat down beside her, and, despite knowing every ugly detail about her life, showed her mercy and compassion. He invited her into a life of abundance and blessing.

This shunned, lonely woman trusted Jesus. She allowed God to bring healing and closure. The same Lord who transformed a broken, untouchable woman into an evangelist—who would bring many others into the same transformative relationship with God—is calling out to you. He knows you're feeling lost, overwhelmed, maybe even cursed. You can choose to trust Him for your life and see where God is taking you next and what He wants you to have.

God knows the enemy is carefully calculating every step and decision you make. With every hope, dream, and desire you have, Satan is strategizing your demise with a well-organized plan to entrap your mind and heart, change your course, and dim the light and hope of your dreams and aspirations. He is at the scene of every crisis, every traumatic event, every sickness, and every failed relationship. He not only hopes that you will not recover, but also tells you that you will never recover. And he never lets you forget that he is available if you want to choose his way.

But God wants to bring you from the heartache and suffering Satan uses to blind you to who you really are: His beloved.

I hope you will see God's personal plan for your life. How God allows you to experience loss, but then restores your heart. How He permits you to live through sickness and be restored. How He allows one door to be closed, but then opens two doors around the corner.

God has already gone ahead to make the path safe for you, and He has given His sweet Holy Spirit to walk alongside you. Walking side by side with the Lord means you are also being followed by peace, grace, and mercy. God shadows us with His Spirit so that we weather the storms of life and come out victorious. The Lord longs to be gracious to you.

I invite you to embark with me on a journey that will not only drastically transform your life, but will also set you on a path that can and will transform the lives of others you meet along the way. As you read, allow God to speak to you through the pages. Workbook sections at the end of each chapter will help you apply these lessons to your life.

I hope this book goes where I can't and does what only God can do in your life. My prayer for you is that the Holy Spirit will meet you where you are, and you will allow yourself to be renewed in Christ.

CHAPTER ONE

Salvation:
Receiving the Gift of Jesus

Jesus told him, "I am the way, the truth, and the life. No one can come to the Father except through me."
—John 14:6 *(NLT)*

Many of us try to understand God's love for man. Even when we turn our back on Him in disobedience and rebellion, He still longs to be with us. God's loves goes beyond comprehension. Salvation is a picture of love that forever seals us to a loving and holy God.

God blesses us each day with gifts and talents, things we need, and even those things we want. Many can agree, and some will argue, that God's timing is rarely when we want it, but always when we need it. But of all the gifts He has given and will give, the one that remains to be the most treasured is the gift of salvation through Christ Jesus. It is life eternal. This gift came with a price no man could purchase because God Himself paid the ransom for. The result is that all of humanity is invited to receive it, and like God, it is always on time.

But sometimes life presents us with challenges.

Psalm 139 gives us a clear picture of the abiding safety we will experience in God's presence when we choose to walk with the Lord:

> *If I go up to the heavens, you are there; if I make my bed in the depths, you are there. If I rise on the wings of the dawn, if I settle on the far side of the sea, even there your hand will guide me, your right hand will hold me fast.*
> **—Psalm 139:8–10**

Here is the assurance of walking with God throughout each season of your life. Nothing you will face will ever take God by surprise. He has gone ahead of you and made provisions for everything you will encounter.

When I was pregnant with my daughter, my doctor placed me on bedrest for my second and third trimesters.. As most mothers do during their pregnancies, I dreamed of what she would look like, what type of personality she'd develop, and what sorts of activities would bring her joy. Even though I hadn't met my daughter yet, I loved her deeply. And even though she didn't know me, I was willing to do whatever it took to protect her—even if that meant giving up some of my freedoms for a time.

My love for my unborn daughter, and my willingness to put her needs before my own, is just a pale comparison to the depth of love God has for each of us. He, too, has dreams for us. He wants to see us grow and flourish. He wants to revel in our pleasures and sit with us in our grief. He wants us to know Him as well as He knows us.

Before we even knew who He was or that our lives

were in danger, He planned to set His rights and privileges aside to save us from certain death. Not the death that ends our physical bodies, which we will all experience, but one that strips the life from our souls.

Jesus' act of self-sacrifice for our sake is what provides salvation.

Unfortunately, God isn't the only one who has a vested interest in the state of our eternal souls. No doubt you've heard of Him. Some call him the devil. Some call him Satan. Whatever name we give him, his purpose is the same: to steal, to kill, and to destroy (John 10:10).

I don't know where you are in your spiritual journey. But I know you picked up this book for a reason. Perhaps you grew up going to Sunday school and hearing stories about David and Goliath (1 Samuel 17) or Jesus' miracle with the loaves and the fish (Matthew 14:13–21). Perhaps you even prayed for Jesus to come into your heart, but then life got in the way of that relationship.

Or perhaps you're just now discovering there is a God who loves you and wants to have a relationship with you. Maybe you want to have a relationship with Him too. You just don't know where to start.

The best place to begin is always the beginning.

What Is Sin?

The LORD God took the man and put him in the Garden of Eden to work it and take care of it. And the LORD God commanded the man, "You are free to eat from any tree in the garden; but you must not eat from the tree of the knowledge of good and evil, for when you eat from it you will certainly die."

—**Genesis 2:15–17**

In the beginning when God created Adam, He gave the man a single job—to safeguard and care for all that God had created (Genesis 2:8–9). But God knew Adam would need help in his task, so He created a helper for Adam: the woman, Eve (Genesis 2:18–22). After giving Adam his charge of responsibility, God told him that they could eat the fruit of any other tree *except* the Tree of Knowledge of Good and Evil (Genesis 2:16–17).

Because Adam was placed in charge of the garden, he was responsible for everything that took place in the garden. That included Eve and the things she would do.

Therefore Satan, who had already declared war on God and His creation, opted to come at Adam from the side instead of launching a frontal attack on the man. He introduced the thought that God was withholding something pleasant and good to Eve, and she, in turn, spread that thought on to Adam.

Contrary to popular storytelling, it wasn't the fruit that was cursed. It was the act. In taking and eating the fruit, Eve and Adam willfully chose to disobey the one law God had given them. The consequence of that choice has affected every human life since.

That's what sin is. A deliberate thought, act, or deed that is contrary to the eternal laws of God. Man's natural inclination to sin is our sin nature. This means we know what God has instructed us to do, but in defiance we choose to do what we want to do. This is man's sinful nature, and it separates us from God. It's a poison that spreads through every aspect of our lives. It fills us with shame, fear, doubt, and greed. It causes us to envy what others have or believe we are superior to those around us. This poison even infects the natural world—both plants and animals.

Like Satan, sin rots, kills, and destroys everything it touches. To stop its spread, we needed a cure. Fortunately, the story doesn't end there. God knew the choice Adam and Eve would make and the path humanity would take. But in His compassion and love, God didn't want our lives to be ruined forever as a result. Remember, nothing surprises God. So before He spoke the first words of creation, God made a plan.

That's where salvation comes in.

What Is Salvation?

For God so loved the world that he gave his one and only Son, that whoever believes in him shall not perish but have eternal life. For God did not send his Son into the world to

condemn the world, but to save the world through him.
—John 3:16–17

To put it simply, salvation takes us from tarnished and stained to shiny and new. God restores us to whom He created us to be and sees the full potential of our being. It is this intended beauty and purpose, which is restored to us through salvation, that we will explore throughout the pages of this book. Salvation offers us a bridge from our sinful nature to a perfect and holy God.

Imagine putting a filthy, smelly garment in the same drawer as your clean clothes. You just wouldn't do it! Instead, you'd make sure the dirty clothing was bleached, washed, and dried so that it was as clean as everything else in the dresser.

Just as a stained shirt cannot clean on its own, we can't remove sin from ourselves. The stain of sin can only be removed by God, and He cleans away our sin through His only Son, Jesus Christ, who knew no sin and was free of blemish.

God is holy—sanctified, hallowed, pure, and sacred—sin and evil cannot exist in His presence. So long as we have the stain of evil and rebellion on us, we cannot be in the same place as Him. As we spend more time studying the Bible, we find that no good works, good deeds, human morality, or religious activity will earn us acceptance with God (Ephesians 2:8–9). In the Old Testament, we see example after example of how impossible it is for us to restore an unhindered relationship with God. As we move into the New Testament, we find that it is through the confession of our faith in Jesus and what He did on the cross that saves us (Romans 10:9–10).

But just as God didn't force Adam to obey Him in the garden, God doesn't force Himself on us now. Going back to our earlier analogy, God freely offers the antidote to sin's poison. But it's up to us whether we'll accept it from Him or not. When we accept that we have done wrong in our lives and admit we need someone else—Jesus—to make things right again, we receive God's gift.

How do we receive God's gift? Even though there are those who say there are many roads to God, the truth is we all must come to God the same way—through confession and repentance.

Confession means we acknowledge we've done wrong and that we cannot live a pure and blameless life.

Repentance means we actively choose to turn away from our old way of thinking and align ourselves with God.

A confession of faith means you believe Jesus went to the cross to give His life for you. It means that you accept that Jesus is God in the flesh and came to earth. You believe He died, was buried, but rose on the third day with all power over sin and death. And through that power, the stain of sin and death's curse is removed from you.

Salvation: God's Plan from the Beginning

Humanity is flawed, but God knows that. He knew we would need a way to come to Him. He knew we needed to know how to love one another and to live out His commands. That's why He revealed a promise to Adam and Eve when he explained the curses they'd brought on themselves (Genesis 3:16–19). Even then, with the shame of their failure fresh on them, God promised Adam and Eve that He would provide salvation for them and their offspring (Genesis 3:15). Shame was never present before Satan introduced it in the garden. But God—who is all-knowing, all-powerful and ever-present came looking for Adam in the cool of the day.

Imagine your children hiding in shame and unable to face you after they've hurt or disobeyed you. But as a parent you're searching because you want to end their shame and assure them you love them. That's what God did through His Son Jesus. Receiving Jesus is receiving the gift of Salvation.

Jesus' crucifixion and resurrection were not a last-minute play by God. Everything God does is predetermined and methodical. And nothing the enemy does takes God by surprise, not even when Eve was convinced to eat of the Tree of Knowledge of Good and Evil. Satan had launched his attack on man, but he wasn't prepared for what God would do in Eden—or at Calvary.

In Eden and at Calvary, innocent blood was shed to atone for, or cover, the failures of humanity (Genesis 3:21; Romans 3:25). Humanity may have fallen into sin, but sin hadn't destroyed God's purpose for creating us. God provided a sacrifice for us. Jesus took our place, freely giving of Himself for all of humanity. We can now freely accept salvation's gift and enter into a relationship with God—entering into His presence with reverence to worship and be in communion with Him. This is the relationship He had with us before man sinned in the Garden of Eden.

He still has work for each of us to do. In the chapters ahead, we'll talk about that more.

Chapter One Questions

Question: How does all sin come back to choosing to disobey God?

_____

_____

_____

_____

_____

_____

_____

_____

_____

_____

_____

Question: Why is Jesus the only answer to humanity's sin problem? Why is this such a hard message for many in our society to accept?

_____

_____

_____

_____

_____

_____

_____

_____

_____

_____

_____

Action: Memorize the verses shared in this chapter to aid you in presenting the gospel. Seek an opportunity to share your testimony with an unsaved friend or relative this week.

Journal Prompt: Write out your salvation testimony. How did you become aware that you were a sinner, and when and how did you trust Christ as your Savior? If you do not have a salvation testimony, or if you are unsure about your salvation, carefully reread this chapter and talk to a trusted Christian leader about how you can know for sure that you are in right relationship with God.

Chapter One Notes

_____

_____

_____

_____

_____

_____

_____

_____

_____

_____

_____

_____

_____

_____

_____

_____

_____

_____

_____

_____

_____

_____

_____

_____

CHAPTER TWO

Baptism: The Old Becomes New

When He had been baptized, Jesus came up immediately from the water; and behold, the heavens were opened to Him, and He saw the Spirit of God descending like a dove and alighting upon Him. And suddenly a voice came from heaven, saying, "This is My beloved Son, in whom I am well pleased."

—Matthew 3:16–17 *(NKJV)*

Salvation and baptism are often spoken of in the same sentence. However, whereas the majority of the church agrees as to what salvation is—the belief that Jesus is Lord, that He died, was buried, and rose again on the third day—baptism can be more of a sticking point for some Christians. Depending on tradition or denomination, baptism might be seen as more symbolic, a representation of a spiritual rebirth or a physical declaration of one's decision to become a follower of Christ. Some denominations baptize infants, while some others wait until individuals can decide for themselves. Some sprinkle, others go for the full dunk.

I think it's important to state that I believe faith in Jesus and what He accomplished on the cross is sufficient for salvation. Christ's sacrifice covers every sin—past, present, and future. Salvation is a gift given freely by God and does not require additional work from us, as Paul tells us in Ephesians 2:8–9. In that light, water baptism—which was carried out by Jesus' disciples and the apostles even after Christ rose from the grave and returned to heaven—becomes an act of love and a tangible reminder of the new life we have been given through Christ's death, burial, and resurrection.

Water Baptism and Baptism of the Holy Spirit

> *As soon as Jesus was baptized, he went up out of the water. At that moment heaven was opened, and he saw the Spirit of God descending like a dove and alighting on him. And a voice from heaven said, "This is my Son, whom I love; with him I am well pleased."*
> **—Matthew 3:16–17**

There are two types of baptism commonly referenced by the church—water baptism and spiritual baptism, or baptism by the Holy Spirit. If you're new to the church or to Christianity, these two phrases could be a little confusing. Entire books have been written on the subject, but I'd like to take a moment to give you a broad overview of the meaning and differences between the two.

Baptism is not an action or ritual that gets you into

heaven—your faith in Jesus Christ as your Savior does that.

Water baptism is described for the first time in Matthew 3, when Jesus was baptized by John the Baptist at the beginning of his earthly ministry. When the disciples were commissioned by Jesus to be his witnesses, water baptism became both a confession of faith as well as a visual representation of the washing away of the old self and the birth of our new identity in Christ. We're given many examples of Christ's followers carrying out Christ's command to spread the gospel to all nations, "baptizing them in the name of the Father and of the Son and of the Holy Spirit" (Matthew 28:19) all throughout the book of Acts (Acts 2:37–41, 8:5–13, 8:35–39, 9:10–18, 10:34–48, 16:30–33, 18:8, and 19:1–6).

Spiritual baptism, or baptism of the Holy Spirit, was first seen on the day of Pentecost when the promised Holy Spirit was given to those who professed Christ as Lord. The presence of the Holy Spirit in our lives is what enables us to experience God, to know His power in our lives, and to complete the work He has prepared for each of us based on the gifts and talents we're born with (Ephesians 2:10).

The moment we accept Jesus as our Savior, the Holy Spirit seals our relationship with God. This means we are eternally bonded with God and nothing in heaven or earth can separate us from God again (Romans 8:38–39). We are marked as belonging to God.

The Holy Spirit also places us in permanent unification and draws us together with other believers to enjoy fellowship with each other as the church (body of Christ).

Through the church, we have partnership in our joys and in our troubles, and we gain fellow workers to come alongside us as we share the gospel to the rest of the world. Baptism can be an occasion to mark and celebrate this special relationship with other believers.

I share these thoughts as a reminder that no matter when or how you were baptized—or even if you haven't yet made the choice of being baptized—your salvation comes from your confession of faith that Jesus is Lord. You need to establish a relationship with God because the gift of salvation comes through the blood of Christ alone. It is eternal and assures us of eternity with God.

Water baptism is a way we celebrate that gift, much like Communion. But just as the bread and wine, or juice, have no value apart from a confession of faith, neither does immersion in the water if we have not yet decided that we believe in the work Jesus accomplished for us on the cross. From the moment we believe in our hearts and are saved, everything we do, including baptism, is an expression of our faith. Water baptism gives us imagery for the new life we receive in Christ, but it is only the beginning.

Romans 6 says we have been united to Christ in death through baptism and this points us to the coming hope of our future resurrection. When we receive the gift of salvation and are united to Christ, we die to the sin that once overcame us. God is calling us to live our lives as an overflow of the realization of who we are in Him. Now, read on and discover the wonders God has in store for you.

Chapter Two Questions

Question: How would you respond to someone who stated that baptism is necessary for salvation? What verses and examples from Scripture refute this idea?

_____

_____

_____

_____

_____

_____

_____

_____

_____

_____

_____

Question: What does it mean to be baptized by the Holy Spirit? What evidences of this do you see in your life?

_____

_____

_____

_____

_____

_____

_____

_____

_____

_____

_____

_____

Action: Talk to the pastor or one of the leaders of your church about how they identify, prepare, and present candidates for baptism.

Journal Prompt: Recall your baptism. What did you understand regarding the significance of the event (as well as its limitations)? What emotions and spiritual commitments surrounded your baptism?

If you were baptized before salvation, pray about being baptized again in the near future as a celebration of

Christ's saving work in your life. If you have never been baptized, speak with a pastor about the possibility of being baptized as an expression of your faith.

Chapter Two Notes

_____

_____

_____

_____

_____

_____

_____

_____

_____

_____

_____

_____

_____

_____

_____

_____

_____

_____

_____

_____

_____

_____

_____

_____

CHAPTER THREE

Made in God's Image

In the beginning was the Word, and the Word was with God, and the Word was God. He was in the beginning with God. All things were made through Him, and without Him nothing was made that was made.
—John 1:1–3 *(NKJV)*

Have you ever looked in a mirror and wondered who in your family tree you look most like? Or where you get your love for music or drawing? Perhaps you wonder who to blame for that extra padding around your middle, or for the allergy that keeps you from enjoying certain foods or flowers.

For some people, those questions are easy to answer. For others, this isn't always the case. Knowing who we are and where we come from is important to all of us, because it gives us an idea of identity. It also helps us understand why we do the things we do or respond to situations in a certain way.

There is another reason beyond your genetics that you

have the interests and physical characteristics that you have. You were specially created by a very creative God who took immense interest in every aspect of every atom He knit together when forming you (Psalm 139:13). This includes how you look, how you feel, and how you respond to the world around you.

When we read the creation account in Genesis, we see God say, "Let *us* make man in *our* likeness" (Genesis 1:26, emphasis added).

The apostle John points back to this event in his Gospel. With his opening words, he reminds us that the declaration in Genesis 1 is a declaration between God the Father, God the Son, and God the Holy Spirit. "*In the beginning was the Word*" (John 1:1).

When I read through this passage, I often imagine what this conversation might have looked like. I can picture God sitting on His throne with Jesus seated just to His right. The world was freshly made and gleamed like an early spring morning when the sun hits the new leaves and petals just so.

I can imagine the birds singing their songs and the squirrels chattering as they chased each other from one branch to another. The fish splashing in the crystalline water as it flowed through the center of a breathtaking garden. But something was missing.

So God looked over to Jesus and said, "Let's make something together. Something that is unlike anything else we've created before. And let's give it our likeness."

I can picture God stepping down from His throne, and, together with Jesus, taking dirt and shaping it into the first man. He crafted the two eyes, the one nose, and a pair of ears. And then, of course, He designed the mouth—not to chew cud or sound mating calls, but to sing, to speak, and to praise. He designed a mind with the ability to reason and a heart to care for others and enter into deep, personal relationships. And He ignited a passion in us for creating new things.

But God didn't stop there. This man wasn't quite complete yet. God bent over the still form and breathed His Spirit into the man, filling him with life—spirit, soul, and blood.

To complete us and to give us an identity that sets us apart from everything else God made, He gave us a piece of *Himself.* Can you imagine what that looked like when God completed His work of creating and shaping man? I believe He observed the creation, smiled, and said: "That's very good."

Your Identity in Christ

Long before [God] laid down earth's foundations, he had us in mind, had settled on us as the focus of his love, to be made whole and holy by his love. Long, long ago he decided to adopt us into his family through Jesus Christ. (What pleasure he took in planning this!) He wanted us to enter into the celebration of his lavish gift-giving by the hand of his beloved Son.
—Ephesians 1:4–6 (MSG)

Like a child stolen from the cradle at birth, many of us grow up without knowing a thing about who we are or where our unique traits come from. And just as a parent would never lose hope that the missing child would be returned home, our heavenly Father keeps calling out into the world so that we might hear His voice and find our way home.

Dear friend, the enemy to the kingdom of God doesn't want you to know your birthrights (Ephesians 3:1–13). He doesn't want you to know you were born into a royal priesthood and that you are a child of the King (1 Peter 2:9). So he bombards you daily with lies, with offensives that break your heart, and distractions that hinder you from knowing the truth of who you are and to whom you belong.

Satan utterly hates man. He is jealous of man and he is out to destroy who we are. Therefore, Satan knows if he can smear and distort the image of God in us—thereby destroying what we know and cutting us off from what we can be—we will live our lives in bondage to sin and death.

This has been Satan's plan since his fall (Isaiah 14:12–15). When we become aware of the knowledge of who God is and the lengths Satan will go to keep us separated from Him, we begin to understand that an all-out war has been waged on us.

Satan will continue to do all he can to keep you distant from God and living in darkness. He will introduce doubt, fear, and distraction that keep you from spending time with God. Whatever *thing* you struggle the most with, be it a fear or an obsession, that is what he'll use as his main method of attack.

He will also try to convince you that sin is okay. He'll attempt to convince you that even though you fall short in a particular area of your life, you're okay because you go to church or because you are a good enough person. Be aware—Satan knows where you are weak

Satan is clever. The weapons he uses, such as depression, anxiety, and low self-esteem, have now become a common struggle for many. Problems of abuse, childhood molestation, cutting, grief, trauma, and substance abuse alter how we see the world. They can become so large a lens that we can't see the truth beyond all the lies.

If you're struggling with self-harm, or thoughts of it, it's important to know that help is available. There's no shame in seeking help. Please know you are precious, and you don't have to face this battle alone. I encourage you to seek professional and medical help as you find your way back to health and wholeness. But I also want you to know you can't treat the symptoms if you don't acknowledge there is an underlying cause. There is a deceptive force operating against you, keeping you from seeing whom God has made you to be—His beloved child.

If you only acknowledge there is a problem and don't apply care to the wound, then your acknowledgment is surface deep at best. Fortunately, the Spirit of God goes beyond the surface. He touches the soul. Where Satan wants to capture and suppress until you are destroyed, God desires to release and heal, allowing you to live in freedom.

Despite what some may mistakenly say, mental health struggles are not sinful. And God certainly doesn't oppose us seeking help when needed. Quite the contrary! He will send people in your life to help when you're struggling. And He will never leave your side (Hebrews 13:5).

You are not a child wandering about helplessly bound

to Satan's lies. God put His breath into you and He promises to never leave you. Christ already won the battle for you and He is your shield (1 Peter 1:3–5). God has placed His Spirit in you and made you His child (Romans 8:14–16), and He will care for you as such.

Your True Identity

> *Finally, be strong in the Lord and in his mighty power. Put on the full armor of God, so that you can take your stand against the devil's schemes. For our struggle is not against flesh and blood, but against the rulers, against the authorities, against the powers of this dark world and against the spiritual forces of evil in the heavenly realms.*
> *—Ephesians 6:10–12*

Even when we experience victory and a freedom from our struggles, Satan is determined to succeed in his attacks. He may leave you for a season, but he will come back like a thief to steal your joy (John 10:10). He'll even use that same issue again during a different season of life when you thought you'd finally gotten past it. Don't be fooled.

Even believers in Christ struggle with their identities and their self-worth Make no mistake, people will label you based on what they see or think they know about you; they are mere instruments in the hands of the enemy, and they don't even know it. He will use the ignorance of others to pull you down and plant seeds of doubt about your character. He will use the ignorance of people to sideline your dreams and deprive the world of your voice and your gifts.

God didn't just say, "Let there be," and, poof, there was a man. No, God intentionally created man in His true image. Man reflects God's likeness because He gave us Himself. For many of us, our identity has been hidden and goes undiscovered for too long. Have you ever been told that you act or look just like your dad or that you remind someone of your mom? That's because you have their DNA and learned mannerisms. The same is true for our spiritual inheritance from our heavenly Father. We have spiritual DNA. We are created in God's likeness so that we can go to Him and communicate with Him and have a relationship built on trust, intimacy, and love. This same spiritual alertness, or discernment, forewarns us when something is not right.

By developing a strong relationship in the Lord and recognizing the power we have in the name of Christ, we can constantly remind ourselves of our true identity in Christ. Like any relationship, our relationship with God isn't one we can will or force to happen. Jesus taught that such a relationship was a gift, a bestowal, or an endowment, freely given by the Father to each of his children who sincerely desires it and who will, in faith, ask for it (Matthew 7:11).

More than anything, God wants to be the lover of your soul. He wants to be on your mind as much as you are on His mind. Will every day be a breeze? Assuredly not! But there is a peace that goes beyond any explanation in the life of the believer (Philippians 4:7), even in the midst of struggles when you come to a place where you can cast all your cares and fears at the feet of our Father (1 Peter 5:7).

You, beloved, have been created in the likeness of God. You, beloved, have been given the gift of salvation. You don't have to struggle to figure out the purpose for your life; simply seek a relationship with the Father who draws your spirit to His Spirit. Jesus came to restore our love and faith in the Father and offer us the gift of eternal life. The enemy may roar and scream and throw every insult in the book at you, but no matter what he'd have you believe, the truth remains—you, beloved, are the image of God.

Chapter Three Questions

Question: How do all destructive behaviors ultimately trace back to an identity problem? How have you seen this in your own life or in the lives of those you know?

_____

_____

_____

_____

_____

_____

_____

_____

_____

_____

_____

_____

Question: How can you cultivate a strong and loving relationship with God that will ground you in your identity in Him? What specific attitudes and actions will lead to this type of relationship?

_____

_____

_____

_____

_____

_____

_____

_____

_____

Action: Reach out to someone who is battling depression or harmful behaviors. Share a Scripture or a thought about their identity in Christ that will encourage them (without sounding "preachy"). Let them know you are praying for them, and if appropriate pray together.

Journal Prompt: What does it mean to you to know that you are made in the image of God? What unique characteristics and gifts reveal the divine stamp on your soul? In what ways have you embraced your identity in Christ, and in what ways have you listened to the enemy's lies and distortions?

Chapter Three Notes

CHAPTER FOUR

The Good Shepherd

I am the good shepherd; I know my sheep and my sheep
know me—just as the Father knows me and I know the Fa-
ther—and I lay down my life for the sheep.
                                                    —John 10:14–15

One of the first hymns I was taught as a child was "In the Garden," which has the refrain, "And He walks with me, and He talks with me, and He tells me that I am His own."[1]

I remember the mood in the church when the mothers would sing this hymn. The passion that came from them as they sang the words felt to me as if they knew God personally. It struck me then and remains with me to this day.

This is a hymn that describes safety, love, and intimacy that can only be experienced through a close and personal relationship with God. Who wouldn't want to know a God who thinks of us with such compassion and detail for our every need?

Gardening and farming are common themes in the

Bible. In John 15:1, Jesus calls Himself the true vine and calls His Father the gardener. He gives parables about farmers and vineyard owners. The people Jesus lived alongside were agrarian and pastoral people, and He often used references and images of familiar topics to convey God's truth. They raised crops. They tended cattle. They also cared for sheep. So, it's really no surprise that He also spoke a number of times about sheep and shepherds. We're a little more removed from fields and flocks these days, especially those of us who live in cities. As a result, some of Jesus' sayings and parables aren't as relatable to us.

In John 10, we see Jesus speaking to a crowd of religious leaders and commoners about sheep, gates, and shepherds. Here, Jesus calls Himself the Good Shepherd. In those times, if a shepherd was faced with a threat to his flock, he put himself between his sheep and the predator if a lion, bear, or wolf suddenly got a hankering for lamb chops and mutton. Additionally, a shepherd slept at the doorway of the sheepfold at night to make sure nothing and no one went in or out of the fold. Including the sheep. So is the same with our Good Shepherd.

I'm reminded of another shepherd who understood what it meant to provide protection for his flock. He's described as small in stature and as a dreamer who loved writing poetry and songs. Though he came from a very humble position and was even overlooked by his family, this young shepherd would grow up to become the fiercest and godliest of Israel's kings.

His name is David, and his story begins in 1 Samuel 16. David had a unique perspective about God and wrote prolifically about his relationship with his heavenly Father. In Psalm 23, David calls God his shepherd and praises Him for caring for each and every one of his needs. When you really understand the great responsibility a shepherd has, you begin to see clearly the care and love that God has for you.

Like the author of "In the Garden," David wrote about how God walked with him, and how God talked with him, and how God told David that he was His own. David had an intimate relationship with the Lord from his early years tending sheep, and the more time David spent with the Lord, the more he learned about God's character. He also learned more of who he was becoming.

The psalms that David wrote allow us to see the imprint God had on his life and the impact He can have on our lives. While they are not in chronological order, we see David's life as a servant, worshipper, warrior, king, husband, and father. We also see the man who messed up in some significant ways, who was grieved by his rebellion against God, and who sought forgiveness and restoration. David understood that to get through every season of life, he needed and wanted the Lord to be his shepherd.

David is like many of us; one moment we are bold and operating in faith and the next we are full of anxieties and doubts. Take for instance, in Psalm 22 David is crying out for help and sounds a little perturbed with the Lord:

> *My God, My God, why have You forsaken Me? Why are You so far from helping Me, and from the words of My groaning? O My God, I cry in the daytime, but You do not hear; and in the night season, and am not silent. ... I am poured out like water, and all My bones are out of joint; My heart*

is like wax; it has melted within Me. My strength is dried up like a potsherd, and My tongue clings to My jaws; You have brought Me to the dust of death.
—Psalm 22:1–2, 14–15 *(NKJV)*

When we read on in Psalm 23, we find a change in David's tune. In his despair, he is reminded of God's goodness and sovereignty. He's reminded that even in the midst of his darkest moments, when David feels that God is absent, He is very much present. So David does what David does best, and he begins to praise the Lord. His prayer of praise has gone on to be one of the most recognizable prayers of the Bible:

The LORD is my shepherd; I shall not want. He makes me to lie down in green pastures; He leads me beside the still waters. He restores my soul; He leads me in the paths of righteousness for His name's sake.

Yea, though I walk through the valley of the shadow of death, I will fear no evil; for You are with me; Your rod and Your staff, they comfort me.

You prepare a table before me in the presence of my enemies; You anoint my head with oil; my cup runs over. Surely goodness and mercy shall follow me all the days of my life; and I will dwell in the house of the LORD forever.
—Psalm 23:1–6 *(NKJV)*

In the middle of his hardship and despair, David reminds himself of five attributes of God:

- *Jehovah-Jireh*, the Lord our Provider (Psalm 23:1)
- *Jehovah-Rapha*, the Lord our Healer (Psalm

23:3a)

- *Jehovah-Tsidkenu,* the Lord our Righteousness (Psalm 23:3b)

- *Jehovah-Shalom*, the Lord our Peace (Psalm 23:4)

- *Jehovah-Shammah*, the Lord Who is Present (Psalm 23:6)

In remembering who the Lord is, David was reminded there was never a time when the Lord did not provide and care for him.

I find great encouragement in this because I, too, face moments in my life when I struggle to see God in the midst of pain, whether it's my pain or the pain of someone I hold dear. Satan will often use these moments as proof that God is absent or unconcerned with our hurts and struggles. He takes our moments of doubt, desperation, and depression and preys on them so that we feel further isolated and abandoned.

David had a close enough relationship with God that he felt safe laying everything out on the line, no matter how ugly it was. But his relationship also shows us that he didn't remain in that painful space. God is well aware of the thoughts we hide from ourselves, and He's not angered by them (Psalm 139:2; Psalm 103:8). By acknowledging them openly and honestly, we allow God to come into our struggle and remind us once again who He is and who we are to Him.

God has personally been and continues to be my Good Shepherd. There have been many seasons of my life when

I didn't quite know what He was doing, but He always came through as my Provider and Healer.

In our struggle to be parents, and with all the things spoken after we lost our second child, I should have been nervous during the next pregnancy. But I believe God was faithful and that He covered my mind and heart in peace during that time. My daughter's birth was a struggle, and she came out with a detached umbilical cord—yet the peace and presence of God was felt in that room as He proved Himself to be Jehovah-Shalom, the bringer of peace.

God's Anointing—an Act of Protection

You prepare a table before me in the presence of my enemies; You anoint my head with oil; My cup runs over.
—Psalm 23:5 *(NKJV)*

Of all the illustrations in this particular psalm, the anointing with oil is the most powerful for me. Many think of an anointing as a spiritual blessing or a gift, and it is in many instances. David himself was anointed with holy oil by Samuel to signify God had set him apart to be Israel's next king. But, when David tell us that his Shepherd anoints his head with oil, he's not talking about his kingship. He's referring back to God's healing and restoration.

I did a little research to understand the relationship and responsibilities of a shepherd to his sheep and discovered at a certain time of the year, when the climate is hot and humid, sheep can become infested and infected by flies, mosquitoes, and other insects—especially around their nose.

Flies seek out the nasal cavity to deposit their eggs on the damp mucous membranes. If these eggs attach and hatch, small parasitic worms will make their way to the sheep's head and burrow into their brain, causing inflammation and severe irritation. Essentially, they drive the sheep mad.

The sheep have no way to escape from this pain, other than hitting or banging their heads or frantically running into things. Some sheep beat their heads against rocks, trees, and posts so severely that they pass out from exhaustion and pain; other sheep may even kill themselves from the thrashing of their heads.

Shepherds of David's day knew this season came every year. Therefore, they prepared a recipe of olive oil mixed with sulphur and spices and anointed the sheep's heads to prevent their sheep from these harmful infestations.[2]

Those flies and parasites are very much like the negative thoughts we all find running rampant through our minds at one point in time or another. Maybe we said something we shouldn't have or didn't say something we should have. Perhaps there's a mistake or blatant wrong we just can't seem to forget about. Or perhaps we haven't done anything wrong per se, but we just can't stop hearing the voice telling us the world is better off without us.

Whatever it is, the words and scenes replay over and over in our head like an obnoxious earworm. It's enough to drive us mad, be it from guilt, shame, regret, or despair.

That's where God comes in.

He knows who His sheep are. He covers us with His

peace and applies His oil until it runs over. No matter where we are or what we've done or not done, like a good shepherd, God doesn't abandon us to the wild. He'll come look for us if we've strayed because we belong to God and it is His joy to care for us.

The final verse of David's psalm reminds us that God's promises are eternal. We who are His cannot be separated from Him any more than He can separate Himself from Himself.

Jesus Is the Good Shepherd

"I am the good shepherd; I know my sheep and my sheep know me—just as the Father knows me and I know the Father—and I lay down my life for the sheep...."

...The Jews who heard these words were again divided. Many of them said, "He is demon-possessed and raving mad. Why listen to him?"

But others said, "These are not the sayings of a man possessed by a demon. Can a demon open the eyes of the blind?"
—John 10:14–15, 19–21

The people listening to Jesus when he called Himself the Good Shepherd would have been very familiar with the words of David and whom those words referred to. There was no doubt in anyone's mind that Jesus was calling Himself God.

For some, His words were the ultimate form of blasphemy and they sought His death. For others, His words brought the hope and healing they'd long been watching for. And when Jesus willingly laid down His life unto death, He gave them life as a shepherd does for his sheep.

As followers of Christ, those words bring us life and hope too. Knowing Jesus is our Shepherd, we should run to Him, seeking all that He has for us because He already knows what we are in need of. We want Him—not just for the oil and ornament, but so that our cups run over. God is the Good Shepherd and He continually tends to His sheep. And if you are a child of God, He calls you His sheep. Knowing this, we can be fully confident that we can cast all our cares upon Him in prayer, knowing He cares for us (1 Peter 5:7).

WORKBOOK

Chapter Four Questions

Question: How does Satan try to use pain in your life to accomplish his purposes? How does God desire to use pain? How can you deal with suffering with both honesty and faith?

_____

_____

_____

_____

_____

_____

_____

_____

_____

_____

_____

Question: What does the shepherd anointing his sheep with oil represent? How has God delivered you from harmful thought patterns? Do you currently struggle with thought patterns where you need His deliverance and peace?

_____

_____

_____

_____

_____

_____

_____

_____

_____

_____

_____

Action: Do a study on the names of God, beginning with the ones listed in this chapter. How do God's names reveal His character and attributes? What do these mean in your own life?

Journal: Think of how God is your Shepherd. How has He and how does He provide for, protect, and anoint you? Like David, express to Him in writing your fears and frustrations, as well as your trust and praise because of who He is.

Chapter Four Notes

_____

_____

_____

_____

_____

_____

_____

_____

_____

_____

_____

_____

_____

_____

_____

_____

_____

_____

_____

_____

_____

_____

_____

CHAPTER FIVE

Prayer—What It Is, Why It Matters

I call on you, my God, for you will answer me; turn your ear to me and hear my prayer.

—Psalm 17:6

Prayer means different things to different people. For some it's just a word we use in the middle of a tragedy to let someone know we are standing beside them from a distance. Some come to it as a form of meditation and personal reflection. For others, it's seen as an obligation or requirement to maintain a right standing with God. And then there are those who turn to it in a moment of desperation, after they have exhausted all other avenues of help.

But what is prayer really? What is its purpose and function in the life of a believer?

Simply put, prayer is an act of worship. For the believer, prayer is powerful and intimate. It's a way we communicate with our heavenly Father. Prayer draws us into a deeper relationship, not just with God but also with the entire body of Christ, the church. When we have a prayer life with the Lord, it is for every season of life and every area of life Prayer humbles us; we see who we are and whom God created us to be when we actively seek time with Him.

When we go before God with the right motives, it put us in direct contact with a holy and sovereign Lord. Jesus said, "Your Father, who sees what is done in secret will reward you" (Matthew 6:6). He told us to go into our room—into our secret place. This makes Satan nervous because the last thing he wants to see is us spending alone time with God. Satan has no access to the secret place.

Prayer is such an important part of our relationship with Christ that Jesus took the time to teach His disciples the proper way to pray

> *This, then, is how you should pray: "'Our Father in heaven, hallowed be your name, your kingdom come, your will be done, on earth as it is in heaven. Give us today our daily bread. And forgive us our debts, as we also have forgiven our debtors. And lead us not into temptation, but deliver us from the evil one.'*
> **—Matthew 6:9–13**

When we look at the Lord's Prayer closely, we see three distinct elements emerge: identity, intercession, and interruption.

Prayer of Identity

Prayer helps us discover our identity in Christ. First, it reminds us of who God is—a good Father who cares for the needs and concerns of his children. Second, it invites God to reveal to us areas of our lives in which we are struggling or failing, as we read in Psalm 139:23–24: "Search me, God, and know my heart; test me and know my anxious thoughts. See if there is any offensive way in me, and lead me in the way everlasting." Finally, prayer equips us to handle the various ups and downs of our day. Through prayer we can cry out to the Creator of the universe to celebrate God's goodness in our lives, when we are treated unfairly or unjustly, or on behalf of others. Having a prayer of identification reveals, shapes, and sustains; a dedicated prayer life invites the search light of the Holy Spirit into our lives.

Prayer of Intercession

Prayer allows us to intercede or intervene for others in their moments of need. Where our natural inclination is to look to our wants and needs first, a deepening prayer life reminds us to think beyond ourselves and consider the needs of those around us—especially those who are fellow members of the family of God.

Paul tells us, "And pray in the Spirit on all occasions with all kinds of prayers and requests. With this in mind, be alert and always keep on praying for all the Lord's people" (Ephesians 6:18). Prayer does what we cannot do, and it goes where we cannot go. The Holy Spirit often brings specific people to mind; sometimes these are people we barely know or rarely see. It's important to recognize this isn't a random occurrence, it's an opportunity to pray on their behalf. This assignment is a holy trust.

The Lord has a reason, often beyond our knowledge, as to why we need to pray for others. Perhaps they're entering into a season of illness or financial hardship. Perhaps the enemy is working overtime in their lives to distract them or discourage them in the Lord's calling. Or this may be the moment the individual on your heart is ready to make a decision to follow Christ, but lacks someone to come alongside to show the way.

Don't dismiss the prompting of the Holy Spirit to pray for those He places on your heart—in your spirit. It could be that from the moment God places someone on your heart, you are being called to offer a kind word, support, trustworthiness, and a prayer.

Prayer of Interruption

Prayer goes beyond expressing our needs and airing our grievances. Prayer interrupts the reign of evil and extends the Kingdom of God to broken people, no matter who they are:

> *It's easy to pray for the people we love, but praying for our enemies is something that's often beyond us—especially when we have suffered harm at the hands of that particular person. But Jesus tells us to do just that: But I tell you, love your enemies and pray for those who persecute you, that you may be children of your Father in heaven. He causes his sun to rise on the evil and the good and sends*

rain on the righteous and the unrighteous.
—Matthew 5:44-45

When we come to a place where we can set aside our rights to demand justice or vengeance, there is a change that takes place in our hearts. This starts the process of restorations of the mind and spirit. It interrupts the enemy's plan to keep you and those who have wronged you separated from God, and it also clears away barriers that keep you from forming a deeper relationship with God.

I've learned a valuable lesson in my spiritual journey with Christ: just because there are some people I don't like, doesn't change the fact that God loves them. He desires to bless their lives just like I want to be blessed. When I release my anger and grudges toward others, I don't just free them—I free myself. And I free God to work in and through me.

He longs to interrupt your life and do the same through you.

The Effectiveness of Prayer

The prayer of a righteous person is powerful and effective.
—James 5:16b

Satan knows how powerful prayer is. He knows this is how we communicate with our Father. He also knows Jesus sits at the right hand of God interceding on our behalf (Romans 8:34). And the enemy is very aware that the Holy Spirit acts as our guide in prayer, even when we don't know what to pray or can't articulate the words:

In the same way, the Spirit helps us in our weakness. We do not know what we ought to pray for, but the Spirit himself intercedes for us through wordless groans. And he who searches our hearts knows the mind of the Spirit, because the Spirit intercedes for God's people in accordance with the will of God.

—Romans 8:26–27

Satan does all that he can to distract us from that power, feeding off our hurts, shame, doubts, and insecurities. One way he does so is by trying to convince us that prayer is ineffective and that God doesn't really hear or answer us when we pray.

Through practice, I learned that one of the most important traits for a counselor is to be a good listener. Prayer, like any form of conversation, is more than just about one person speaking and another listening and responding with action. Listening is an active part of communicating. When we pray and seek God's heart, we should listen for the voice of God to better understand His will and His instructions.

Too often we run through a list of things we want God to do for us and call them prayer requests. But when those requests aren't answered when and how we want, then we give up on praying and on God.

God places promises in our hearts that may take a lifetime to be fulfilled. There are others we may never live to see to fruition, but the generations behind us will. I think of Abraham and Sarah waiting past the point of hope for their promised son Isaac (Romans 4:18). I think of grandmothers who pray for the revival of a generation that has yet to be conceived. And I think of men and women living in countries where they can't pray openly, yet they continue to wait expectantly for the day they can praise the Lord in public without risk of imprisonment or death.

God is faithful to the prayers of His people, and He opens doors of opportunity for you. Most of us are living out the things we asked God for, yet have never said "thank You." But prayer is effective and shows how God listens. When we go before the Lord with an understanding of who He is and who we are— knowing our prayers are heard and willing to listen to the Lord's response—our prayers are powerful, effective, and ultimately life-changing.

The Heart of a Prayer Warrior

I have been blessed to be around people who can captivate the room just by walking in. They bring and leave peace with them that sets my mind and spirit at rest. These are people who are serious about prayer because they're serious about their relationship with God. They speak to Him and more importantly, they listen to Him.

We often call people like this prayer warriors. This isn't a title that is limited to people who have everything in their life put together or to Christians who've walked with God for decades. Anyone who has put their faith in Christ can be a prayer warrior, including you.

The heart of a prayer warrior desires the will of God be made known in the lives of those they are praying for. They stand believing God for salvation, healing, physical and spiritual breakthrough, even when the person they're praying for feels like giving up. They come alongside the hurting and wounded and say, "I'm going to see this thing through with you." They don't shy away from a fight with spiritual forces.

The heart of a prayer warrior is strengthened and emboldened by the Holy Spirit to speak up against the darkness pressing in on the world around us. The Spirit also reveals our Father's compassionate heart and His desire to bring hope and restoration to those lost in the darkness. When you pray, listen for His voice. Perhaps the Lord is asking you now: "Will you be that light?"

Prayer brings about a relationship with God when you intentionally invite Him to reign over your life in every area. Knowing God and being in a relationship with Him means you're walking with Him daily, asking for direction and guidance, giving Him praise and honor, or spending time in the serenity of His Presence.

For me, it is a blessing to spend time in the Lord's presence and experience an atmosphere of worship. My prayer time with the Lord allows me to rest in His presence, in awe and reverence of who He is.

Take comfort in knowing that your prayers are effective—and that He hears you.

Chapter Five Questions

Question: What misconceptions about prayer hinder your prayer life? What distractions keep you from prayer? Do you see yourself as a *prayer warrior*? Why or why not; if not, what will it take to become one?

_____

_____

_____

_____

_____

_____

_____

_____

_____

_____

Question: Are your prayers balanced—that is, do you incorporate worship, repentance, intercession, listening, etc. into your prayer time, or do your prayers sound like a spiritual (or selfish!) wish list? Which areas need more focus and which need less? What things are you praying for that will have an impact beyond your own lifetime?

_____

_____

_____

_____

_____

_____

_____

_____

_____

_____

_____

Action: There are many different types of prayer systems that can be helpful in interceding, realizing God's answers to prayer, and keeping His character and faithfulness in the forefront of your prayers. Set up a system that will help you and encourage you to be faithful and consistent in prayer.

Alternately, interview someone in your church who is known as a *prayer warrior*. Ask for advice on how you can grow in your prayer life.

Journal Prompt: Plan a prayer retreat—a day or half a day when you can be alone with God, your Bible, and your journal. Decide on one or two issues close to your heart that you will focus on for your prayer time.

Chapter Five Notes

_____

_____

_____

_____

_____

_____

_____

_____

_____

_____

_____

_____

_____

_____

_____

_____

_____

_____

_____

_____

_____

CHAPTER SIX

Authentic Praise and Worship

In that day you will say: "Give praise to the LORD, proclaim his name; make known among the nations what he has done, and proclaim that his name is exalted. Sing to the LORD, for he has done glorious things; let this be known to all the world."

—Isaiah 12:4–5

If you've spent any amount of time in church, you've no doubt become familiar with what is generally called praise and worship. Generally speaking, it's a time of singing, praying, and the passing of the offering plate prior to the pastor stepping up behind the pulpit to preach. But authentic praise and worship are so much more!

Consider this: A soldier on the battlefield places himself in harm's way to protect his fellow soldiers or defenseless innocents trapped by enemy fire. A doctor and her team stand on their feet for thirty-six hours, tirelessly working to save the life of a child born with a rare heart defect. A custodian gives twenty years of service maintaining a school so that the teachers and students have a clean and safe environment.

When we recognize these actions and offer our gratitude and thanks to these individuals for their sacrifice and hard work, we call it praise. That's what praise is—the thankful acknowledgment of another's generous and selfless acts.

Praise is something all of us desire in our lives. Not because we are selfish or egotistical, but because we genuinely want to be seen and want our hard work to be recognized. We desire praise because God desires praise. By extension, authentic worship is an elevated form of praise. In fact, when we *worship* God, we are elevating Him above everything else in our lives. We are declaring that He is praiseworthy and deserving of the highest honor. Not because of what He's done, but because of who He is. The holy and unchanging Creator of all things.

Don't be surprised if, when you offer God your true praise and worship, you find yourself feeling tired and worn out. I've discovered that moments of authentic praise can be like getting up first thing in the morning and working out. I might be sweating after I'm done, but it sure feels good afterward!

Authentic Praise Is More than a Happy Feeling

My sin, oh, the bliss of this glorious thought! My sin, not in part but the whole, is nailed to the cross, and I bear it no more; praise the Lord, praise the Lord, O my soul![3]

Authentic praise and worship recognizes our brokenness and God's holiness. It acknowledges our need for a Savior, not just at the moment we first believe in Jesus as the Son of God, but every day afterward. Authentic praise and worship returns us again and again to the gospel and the work God has promised to complete in our lives as Paul described in Philippians 1:6 "...that he who began a good work in you will carry it on to completion until the day of Christ Jesus."

Authentic praise and worship goes beyond how we feel in a given moment. In fact, some of the most authentic moments of worship come in the midst of our deepest heartache and anguish. We need only look to the Psalms to see examples of a man struggling with depression and anxiety, but who chooses to praise in the midst of his darkest moments.

King David and the rest of the psalmists aren't alone in this. One of the most powerful and enduring hymns of praise penned in the late 19th century was written by a man who had, like Job, lost his family and wealth and was considered by some as cursed by God because of a secret sin. And yet, as Horatio Spafford passed near the spot where his daughters had drowned in a shipwreck and his wife alone was saved, he began praising the Lord for His mercy and goodness.[4]

In the words of his hymn "It Is Well with My Soul," Spafford acknowledges his pain and grief, but he doesn't end there. Instead, he turns his eyes to the One God who redeems and restores and makes right.

Authentic worship tells the story of what you have been through. It is born out of your personal experiences.

It pushes past people and their expectations, reaching down into your soul and relinquishing power and authority to God to restore and make whole what was broken.

Authentic Praise and Worship Keep Us Humble

> *To some who were confident of their own righteousness and looked down on everyone else, Jesus told this parable: "Two men went up to the temple to pray, one a Pharisee and the other a tax collector."*
> **—Luke 18:9–10**

Authentic praise and worship acknowledges our constant need for the Lord's continual presence in our lives. In Romans 8, Paul writes about the inner struggle we face every day to do what is right in God's eyes. He writes:

> *For in my inner being I delight in God's law; but I see another law at work in me, waging war against the law of my mind and making me a prisoner of the law of sin at work within me. What a wretched man I am! Who will rescue me from this body that is subject to death? Thanks be to God, who delivers me through Jesus Christ our Lord!*
> **—Romans 7:22–25a**

We see examples of this struggle every day in our lives and, unfortunately, in the lives of men and women who have been placed in roles of authority inside and outside of the church. Authentic praise reminds us that we still live in a fallen world and face the temptation to put ourselves above God. Authentic praise and worship reminds us that while we still struggle and make mistakes, God cares for us and cared enough about us that He made a way for us to come to Him in our weakness long before we even knew we had a problem.

Authentic praise and worship reconnects us to the Father and the Son through the Holy Spirit, and it allows us to enter into a deeper relationship with God. It allows us to bring our needs before the throne and to hear God's answer to our petition. It also empowers us to go out into the world and use the gifts and talents we were born with for God's glory.

Ultimately, authentic praise and worship brings us into the very relationship Jesus spoke of when He spoke to His disciples and followers about abiding in Him (John 15:1–17).

What Authentic Praise and Worship Looks Like

Praise the LORD. Praise God in his sanctuary; praise him in his mighty heavens. Praise him for his acts of power; praise him for his surpassing greatness.
—Psalm 150:1–2

Authentic praise comes from the heart. It can be as simple as saying thank you for little things like your morning cup of coffee or tea, for having a car that starts, or for arriving safely at work. It can be saying thank you for an unpleasant experience that prevented you from making a bigger mistake later on. It might even be acknowledging that although you wish you were free from whatever suffering you're experiencing in this moment (sickness, depression, or financial ruin), you're breathing today because God still has a purpose for you on this earth—even if you don't know what it is yet. Authentic worship tells the story of what you have been through; it is born out of your experiences. Authentic praise and worship pushes past people. In a way, it is us relinquishing any control we think we have, asking God to be in charge and intervene on our behalf.

Authentic worship is sometimes expressed privately in a locked room on your knees pouring your heart out to God. It's sometimes public, openly weeping, waving hands, or dancing. We don't do these things to draw attention to ourselves, but because we are genuinely overwhelmed with gratitude for God's mercy in our lives. When we truly praise the Lord and give Him the worship He rightly deserves, we don't just honor Him. We reclaim who we were created to be.

When we worship Him, it creates an atmosphere that Satan and his army can't enter into. Satan knows this. He knows what worship does, therefore he is relentless in his pursuit to disrupt your worship. He'll whisper fears into your ear to distract you. He'll fill your mind with your to-dos and have-nots.

The last thing he wants is for you to experience the freedom and wholeness that authentic praise and worship brings into your life. This is why it is so important that we guard our worship, whether it be praying, singing, meditating on Scripture, or coming together with other believers. Satan knows that when we continually enter into genuine worship and praise, the distractions this world offers to keep our eyes off God become less appealing. When we worship, we begin to recognize that for all their flashing lights and promises of fulfillment, the things of this world really are just empty husks.

So why is authentic praise and worship so valuable? It doesn't just honor God and give Him the glory He deserves. It also guards our hearts and lives from things that promise to give us life but bring only death instead (Philippians 4:8–9).

God does not need our worship, but it should be our diligent, heartfelt, reasonable honor to worship a God who knows all our faults but still redeems us, chooses us, and calls us *beloved*. Our sincere worship and praise offers a sweet fragrance unto the Lord because He created us to give Him glory, to worship and adore Him, and to be in a relationship with Him.

WORKBOOK

Chapter Six Questions

Question: Describe a time when you experienced authentic worship borne out of personal suffering. How did praising God change your perspective on your pain?

_____

_____

_____

_____

_____

_____

_____

_____

_____

_____

_____

_____

_____

Question: List some of the benefits of authentic worship in a believer's life, both individually and corporately as a church. Are you seeing these benefits in your life—and why or why not?

_____

_____

_____

_____

_____

_____

_____

_____

_____

_____

_____

_____

Action: Research the life of a great Christian musician (past or present). How were this person's songs the fruit of authentic worship in their own life?

Journal Prompt: While worship incorporates so much more than music, music is a vital expression of worship.

Looking over your life and Christian walk, what song(s) characterizes your walk with Him? What songs have helped you through difficult times or expressed the joy in your heart? Write out the lyrics and describe how that song(s) speaks to you or reflects your relationship with God.

Chapter Six Notes

CHAPTER SEVEN

The Threshing Floor

His winnowing fork is in his hand, and he will clear his
threshing floor, gathering his wheat into the barn and
burning up the chaff with unquenchable fire.
—Matthew 3:12

Threshing is a harvest-time activity when the grain is removed from the husk and the tares, or false grain). The grain is saved, but the husk and tares, or chaff, are not. During Bible times the threshing floor was flat and hardened by the passing of oxen that sometimes pulled a sled over the sheaves of grain to separate the grain from the husks. After the threshing process, the stalks and grain were thrown up into the air so that the wind might blow the unwanted chaff away and leave the valuable kernels. This was known as winnowing. Anything unwanted that remained afterward, such as the sheaves, was thrown into the fire.[5]

God works in a similar way in the lives of His children—coming to the threshing floor is part of your identity as His beloved. In fact, it is proof that God is at work in your life. Your heavenly Father knows you intimately, and He knows what you need; He knows what needs to be removed from your life, so you can be your best self.

Beyond the physical, the threshing floor can also represent a place of blessing and judgment. In Numbers 18:30, the threshing floor is referred to as a place of increase for the freed Hebrew slaves journeying toward God's promise. In Joel 2:24, it depicts a time of prosperity for Israel after a period of correction and repentance.

But judgment occurred on the threshing floor when God issued judgment on Israel as a result of David relying on the strength of his army. David had pride in his great army. He took attention away from what the Lord was doing by attempting to rely on his own resources and by counting his soldiers as the measure of his strength (2 Samuel 24:9). He took his eyes away from what God was doing and as soon as he got the number, guilt set in and immediately he knew that what he had done was wrong. David operated outside of God's will, and as a result the people suffered judgment (see 2 Samuel 24).

God sent the prophet Gad to David to pronounce judgment, but He also gave instructions. God's instructions always provide a way of escape. David followed the instructions given by Gad. He sought out a threshing floor to build an altar. Interestingly, the owner wanted to bless King David by giving him the land. But David refused. He understood he had to purchase the floor in order to own the place where the altar and a sacrifice of prayer would be offered. He would not give to God what cost him

nothing, and a sacrifice cost something. Being intentional about spending intimate time with God is a sacrifice because we have so many things that compete for our time. But nothing is more satisfying than getting in the presence of God and allowing Him to separate the husk from the wheat. Throughout Scripture the threshing floor is used to give us clarification of unusable versus usable and of old versus new.

During His ministry, Jesus uses the threshing floor to depict the separating and purging of the repentant sinner from the unrepentant sinner (Matthew 3:12). Wherever you are and whatever you are holding on to that God has instructed you to release and trust to Him, release it and watch the hand of God move because of your obedience and sacrifice. God's plan for David was to mature him spiritually; and just like God had a plan to spiritually mature and bless David, He desires to bless us too.

If we've come to the cross and accepted Christ as our Savior, we don't have to worry about being cast to the wind like dead husks. But God can and does enter into our lives to separate what is good and holy from what is sinful and dangerous to us. So, what does that look like?

Threshing: Pressed, but Not Crushed

We are hard pressed on every side, but not crushed; perplexed, but not in despair...
—2 Corinthians 4:8

When we go through difficult seasons, it's common to

feel pressed and crushed. Sometimes the situations are of our own making—a lapse in judgment resulting in unforeseen consequences or a habitual sin has finally come to light. Other times, as hard as we look at our lives, we can't find what we did wrong to deserve the pain, sickness, or ruin we are facing.

Where do you turn first in those moments? The honest answer to that question reveals where you put your faith, your hope, and your trust.

These times of pressing may very well be a season of God separating the grain from the husk in your life. The husks may be unhealthy relationships or behaviors that prevent you from being who God has called you to be. They may be careers or finances that give you a false sense of security so that you don't feel the need to depend on God to meet your daily needs.

Ultimately, the husks in our lives can be anything and everything we put before our relationship with God. And we might never have realized we were setting these things up as idols in our lives had God not brought us into a season of threshing.

The beautiful thing about the threshing process is that despite the pressure being placed upon the unseparated grain and husks on the threshing floor, only the husks are broken away. The grain itself is left whole and ready for use. Do not fear being crushed or destroyed during your threshing seasons, dear friend. They are merely times to cleanse and strip away things in your life that are holding you back from being the person God designed you to be.

Purified, but Not Destroyed

Shadrach, Meshach and Abednego replied to him, "King Nebuchadnezzar, we do not need to defend ourselves before you in this matter. If we are thrown into the blazing furnace, the God we serve is able to deliver us from it, and he will deliver us from Your Majesty's hand. But even if he does not, we want you to know, Your Majesty, that we will not serve your gods or worship the image of gold you have set up."

—Daniel 3:16–18

There's a reason why we have sayings like "out of the frying pan and into the fire" or "trial by fire." There are seasons in life where it just seems like we go from one trouble to the next. And each one seems harder than the last.

Fire is a powerful force, but it doesn't have to be a destructive one. Fire also purifies and brings life. Metalsmiths use fire to melt down silver and gold in unimaginably hot flames to remove any impurities and other forms of metal that might be mixed in with them. In Western America, Redwood trees tower high over the forests. Some of them are believed to have sprouted at the time Christ was born.

But not one of them would have seen the light of day had it not been for a fire that burned the seed cone and germinated the seed. In a similar way, God uses His holy fire to clean, purify, and bring life to His children and those who are watching them.

The Old Testament book of Daniel offers a story of which I'm often reminded during seasons of trouble.

Daniel and three of his friends—Shadrach, Meshach, and Abednego—were among the Jewish captives dragged away from Judah to Babylon and into captivity (Daniel 1:3–7).

Not only were they taken away from their homes, but they were also taken away from the temple. Their names were changed by their captors to indicate that their God had fallen to Babylon's gods. But Daniel and his friends refused to waver in their faith. Daniel would be sent to the lion's den and walk out unscathed. Shadrach, Meshach, and Abednego would face a fire so hot that the guards who threw them into the furnace were burned and killed by the flames, but the three Jewish young men weren't even singed. In fact, as the king watched he saw not three but four men walking around in the fire, and he declared that the fourth man looked like "a son of the gods" (Daniel 3:25).

That story is more than a story to me. It's a reminder that whatever I am facing and will face, God will be there to see me through the crushing, the pounding, and the fire. God does not delight in the crushing and pounding, but He knows it is a necessary purifying process to weed out that which is good in our lives from that which is harmful or of no use to us.

The Ongoing Process of Sanctification

When we come to the cross, we are forgiven for all sins—past, present, and future. But God's work in us doesn't stop there. Rather, it's just the beginning of God's threshing work in our lives to remove the sin and purify us.

Perhaps you've heard the words "justification" and "sanctification" during a sermon or while reading a book like this. If you're not familiar with these words yet, *justification* is what happens when we acknowledge our sin and inability to cover the debt we owe God. When we accept that Christ is the one and only atonement needed to cover our sins, we go from being condemned by sin to being justified by Christ. Simply put, justification means we are in right standing with God.

Sanctification, on the other hand, is an ongoing process in the heart of the believer. It is through this process that we are made more Christlike. Sanctification is the believer's threshing floor; it's where God separates the "wheat" from the "chaff" in our lives. It can seem painful and impossible at times, especially when we continue to hold tightly to the things God knows that needs to be removed from our lives.

But ultimately God walks us through seasons of pressing, separation, and fire because of His great love for us. Don't fear to step onto His threshing floor, dear friend. It's for your benefit and it's meant to bring you an abundance of life. When you turn to God during those pressing times and meet with Him in the secret place, He will produce lasting fruit in your life.

WORKBOOK

Chapter Seven Questions

Question: How is a difficult season in a believer's life like a threshing floor? Describe a time when you felt "pressed and crushed." To what person or activity did you turn to first for help and hope?

_____

_____

_____

_____

_____

_____

_____

_____

_____

_____

Question: What are some husks that God has separated or that He desires to separate from the good grain in your life? How will removal of these things make you more like Him and more useable for Him?

_____

_____

_____

_____

_____

_____

_____

_____

_____

_____

_____

Action: Study the life of Joseph, Job, David, Paul, or a similar Bible character who endured great suffering. Which parts of their suffering were brought on by their own sin, and which were caused by others' sin? Trace this character's personal and spiritual growth through the difficulties he or she encountered. What can you learn from them?

Journal Prompt: Write out a prayer to God expressing your commitment to endure and to trust Him through the threshing floor and the fires in your life. Be honest about your feelings, doubts, and fears, but reaffirm your belief in God's loving, good plan for your life.

Chapter Seven Notes

_____

_____

_____

_____

_____

_____

_____

_____

_____

_____

_____

_____

_____

_____

_____

_____

_____

_____

_____

_____

_____

_____

_____

_____

CHAPTER EIGHT

The Secret Place

He that dwelleth in the secret place of the most High shall abide under the shadow of the Almighty. I will say of the LORD, He is my refuge and my fortress: my God; in Him will I trust. Surely He shall deliver thee from the snare of the fowler, and from the noisome pestilence. He shall cover thee with His feathers, and under His wings shalt thou trust: His truth shall be thy shield and buckler.
—***Psalm 91:1–4*** *(KJV)*

Everyone goes through seasons of increased busyness. Work requires more hours. Children require more attention. Events and activities pile up on each other. The fridge is empty and there is a pile of dirty laundry staring at you. And you don't even want to do the things on the to-do list that is growing faster than you can cross off items. So, you plop down on your bed every night and think, "I just need a break from it all!"

It's during these seasons we tend to opt out of spending quiet time alone with God. Instead of seeing it as a time of refreshment and restoration, we see yet another demand for our time. Dear friend, believe me when I say it's in these moments we most need that quiet time with God.

God understands the chaos and the voices clamoring for our attention. He knows what it's like to have people press in on all sides, begging, pleading, and accusing. I imagine that the voices of the multitudes following Him around Judea were deafening. It's no wonder that after feeding the five thousand, He sent His disciples on ahead so He could have a quiet moment to Himself (Matthew 14:23). But when Jesus went up on the mountainside, it wasn't to turn off His brain and unwind. It was to enter into the secret place and spend time in the quiet with His heavenly Father.

The term secret place comes from the Hebrew word *sether* (say-ther), which means "covering, shelter, hiding place, or secrecy."[6] The psalmist wrote, "For in the time of trouble He shall hide me in His pavilion; in the secret place of His tabernacle He shall hide me; He shall set me high upon a rock" (Psalm 27:5 NKJV).

I believe the secret place is more than a location—it's an experience. In Matthew 6:6, Jesus gives us instruction to go into our secret place and shut the door. He wants us to experience what happens when we shut out the things that distract our mind and prevent us from completely setting our eyes on the Lord.

When the psalmist refers to a refuge, I believe he is pointing to a state of peace, acceptance, safety, revelation, and protection that comes when we dwell in God's presence. As Jesus did, we all need a moment of separation.

What are we separating from? Sometimes it is a person, place, or a particular thing—whatever is causing distress in your life. When we become stressed, frustrated, or irritated, it becomes like a grit of sand in our shoe. At first, we ignore it and try to press on, but after a while of it rubbing, our foot gets blistered and raw. Instead of seeing the beauty around us, we can focus only on the irritant that's slowly driving us mad.

When we allow ourselves to step out of the situation that is causing us stress and into God's presence, we're able to realign our hearts and vision with Him. For this reason, in our times in the secret place, with no one else but God, our perspective can be changed drastically. This time with God can help us improve our attitude and behavior toward the person or thing, or it will show us that change or a complete separation is needed.

The Secret Place Brings Transformation

Do not conform to the pattern of this world, but be transformed by the renewing of your mind. Then you will be able to test and approve what God's will is—his good, pleasing and perfect will.
—Romans 12:2

It's impossible to enter into the presence of a Holy God without being changed by the encounter. The more time we spend one-on-one with the Father, the more we begin to resemble Him. But the reverse is also true. The more time we spend away from the Father and entrenched in the world, the less we look like Him.

Even the people who seem like the godliest of people can take on values that don't even resemble godliness.

And I get it, we all want to fit in. We live in a world where if you don't adapt to the world's belief system, you are labeled as a nonconformist, intolerant, or discriminator. This can further fuel frustration and cause disconnections with the God who pursues you.

We're instructed not to be conformed to this world, but to be renewed daily by spending time with God. This can be difficult for many of us because we have chosen to conform. We still care about and want to control how others see us.

Let me help you with something: you can't stop people from thinking what they want to think of you. And no matter what you do or how hard you try, there's always going to be someone who thinks poorly of you. I've concluded that their opinion of me is none of my business. But God sees us all as precious and valued, and his view never changes.

But you won't discover that for yourself unless you spend time alone with Him in your secret place.

The Secret Place Brings Restoration

Though you have made me see troubles, many and bitter, you will restore my life again; from the depths of the earth you will again bring me up.
—Psalm 71:20

Entering into the secret place allows God to reveal the secrets we keep from ourselves, whether they're deep hurts we haven't faced yet or issues with sin we've yet to acknowledge. This isn't meant for our harm or destruction, but rather it's meant for our healing.

The Holy Spirit is the Great Responder who provides and applies the ointment that heals all wounds, those self-inflicted and the ones inflicted by others. But He can only do so when we allow Him.

King David was well aware of this process. When He sinned against God by taking another man's wife and then ordered that man's death to cover up his sin, he didn't just wound the people around him (2 Samuel 11:1–17). He wounded himself and his relationship with God. And even after he confessed his sin and came back into right standing with God, the consequences of his actions followed him (2 Samuel 12:11–14). Healing came, but there were scars left behind.

This happens in the lives of modern-day believers too. We will experience tragic events and come to a point where we are still standing but running on empty. And we'll question why God is allowing such hard, bitter things to enter into our lives. We may even question if He still cares.

Dear friend, He cares deeply. I can't speak to all things, but if you find yourself in this place, maybe it's that you are in a season of life where you need to be spiritually renewed in your faith, in your thinking, and in how you seek and see God for your strength and restoration.

The Secret Place Restores Strength

I know what it is to be in need, and I know what it is to have plenty. I have learned the secret of being content in any and every situation, whether well fed or hungry, whether

living in plenty or in want. I can do all this through him
who gives me strength.
—Philippians 4:12–13

When we spend time in the secret place, we are reminded that we cannot face life and all its complications
by ourselves. This life was meant to be lived in partnership. We cannot forget that we were born into a world at
war. This foe wants to remain hidden, so you think you
are safe walking down the road alone and unarmed. Well,
the enemy does exist and is not hidden; this assailant is
Satan.

Alone we are not a match to fight against the guiles of
the enemy. But God has not left you unequipped for this
fight. He has given you all the equipment you need to
stand against the powers of darkness. But it is impossible
to wield the armor in your own strength. This is why the
Apostle Paul wrote in Ephesians 6:10 to "be strong in the
Lord and in his mighty power," before he described the
armor of God in the verses that followed.

When we enter into the secret place, it's like entering
into a secret gym in which your trainer is a heavyweight
who has never lost a fight. When we enter into this space,
we allow God to enter into our lives. And when the relentless enemy attempts to throw a punch at us, our trainer is
standing behind us to cover our back and direct our coun-
ter-attack so that the enemy is driven back once more. Our
trainer gives us the strength to face the enemy.

The Secret Place Brings Surrender

Finding the secret place isn't hard. It's just a matter of focusing our prayer lives and being willing to give everything to God. Dear friend, if we are going to live our most victorious lives, we have to shift our mindset about who God is and who we are to Him.

Too often, we are oblivious to the importance of prayer in our lives. We think people are dismissing our concerns when they tell us to pray, or perhaps we are the ones dismissing their requests to pray with us. Too often we reside in our pain. We want sympathy instead of solutions. We operate out of our self-interested motives so that when we are given wise counsel, we generally don't apply it. Why is that?

When we come to a place where we recognize we can do nothing apart from God as John 15:5 tells us, we discover the power that comes from seeking a deep, intimate, and abiding relationship with Him. But that won't happen until we are completely honest and vulnerable before God, holding nothing back.

When we seek God and His heart, then prayer, praise, and worship become a continual conversation we have with our Father anywhere and anytime. What was once a chore becomes a joy because in seeking God you'll discover a retreat and safe haven, a welcome respite in life's daily noise. Be renewed and stop the hands of destruction while you build your faith in God. The secret place of the Most High God is where you will be renewed and strengthened in God's arms. It is in the secret place that

God can change your heart and make you more like Him. There you will find grace to face challenges in your life.

Chapter Eight Questions

Question: What internal and external hindrances keep you from the secret place of fellowship with God? What stresses and frustrations in your life point to your need to refocus and realign your heart through this uninterrupted communion with God?

_____

_____

_____

_____

_____

_____

_____

_____

_____

Question: In what ways are you concerned with others' opinions and perceptions of you? What image are you trying to portray to the world? Is this image compatible with the values and image of Christ that God wants you to reflect? If not, in what ways is it different?

_____

_____

_____

_____

_____

_____

_____

_____

_____

_____

_____

Action: Create a poster or sign with a picture of an ancient fortress and a verse about God being your fortress. Include the words "transformation," "restoration," "strength," and "surrender." Place your sign where it will remind you of the need to run to your secret place on a daily basis.

Journal Prompt: A journal can be a record of your time with God in the secret place. If you have never kept a journal, now is a good time to start.

Jot down verses, thoughts, prayers, and Spirit-led impressions. If you are already keeping such a journal, are you being consistent in using it as part of your quiet times with God? Even one to two sentences a day can help to solidify what God is teaching you.

Chapter Eight Notes

CHAPTER NINE

God Hears You—
He Sees You, Too

It so happened that as [Hannah] continued in prayer be-
fore GOD, Eli was watching her closely. Hannah was
praying in her heart, silently. Her lips moved, but no sound
was heard. Eli jumped to the conclusion that she was
drunk. He approached her and said, "You're drunk! How
long do you plan to keep this up? Sober up, woman!"
—1 Samuel 1:12–14 (MSG)

Hannah had a problem. She was a woman living in a society that placed the full value of a woman's worth on her ability, or inability, to provide her husband with a son, and she couldn't get pregnant. Hannah's husband had another wife at the same time who had plenty of children. So clearly the problem lay at Hannah's feet. And the second wife made sure she felt every measure of her shame.

So Hannah went to the Lord and cried out in her grief and despair. Unfortunately, the priest who saw her praying made a quick assumption about her condition. Instead of taking the time to listen and bring words of comfort to a grieving woman with an invisible health condition, he immediately accused her of wrongdoing and of living a sinful life.

Sadly, for all our advancements in science, technology, and understanding of the illnesses that afflict people, Hannah's story is far too common. I've experienced the shame that comes from the stares at the rashes covering my body caused by sarcoidosis. I've felt the soul-crushing pain that came when my husband and I were accused of having a secret sin in our lives after we experienced our second miscarriage within a year of the first.

Chances are you've experienced something similar in your life. Perhaps, like Hannah, you've spent years praying for God to step into your situation and to bring healing or restoration. But maybe you didn't get the answer you were looking for. The enemy of your soul would have you believe it's because God doesn't see your distress or care about your pain.

Dear friend, that's anything but true. No matter where you are or what you are doing, God does see you. He hears you too.

You Aren't Invisible To God

Jesus entered Jericho and was passing through. A man was there by the name of Zacchaeus; he was a chief tax collector and was wealthy. He wanted to see who Jesus was, but because he was short he could not see over the crowd. So he ran ahead and climbed a sycamore-fig tree to see him, since Jesus was coming that way.

—Luke 19:1–4

No one likes a tax collector. Especially when the tax collector is a cheat working for a government you don't like. That was exactly the case for Zaccheus. To the Jews, he would have been considered the lowest of low, a traitor to his people. Someone not worthy of God's notice. And yet, he wanted to see Jesus and was determined not to be pushed out of the way.

So he climbed a tree to see over the crowd, but being in the tree also kept him distant. Perhaps he even felt invisible or wished he could be. After all, if anyone saw him and recognized him, surely he would have been driven away with curses and shouts.

We humans like to put things in nice, neat categories—especially other humans. So we make our lists and label every broken person we meet: angry, depressed, complainer, adulterer, hypochondriac, liar, drunk, cheat, sinner.

The enemy wants you to see yourself as sick, wounded, broken, and valueless because he wants to keep you blind to how the God of the universe sees you. If he can get you to accept those labels, then he can manipulate how you treat others, and, more importantly, how you treat yourself. When you accept the lies as truth, you are effectively sidelined from the work God has prepared for you. He can use you no matter what you live with physically, emotionally, or mentally.

The label the world, and sadly the church, has placed on you is not what God sees when He looks at you. There's only one label that comes to mind when God looks at His children—beloved.

You, dear friend, are the beloved child of God.

Don't allow what you are going through to keep you from pressing through the crowd to see God. And don't allow the unwarranted words of others to come between you and the presence of the Father.

He hears your cry and knows what you need. He sees you, too, just as he saw Zacchaeus hiding in a tree because he couldn't break through the crowd. Jesus didn't just see Zacchaeus, He told him to come down and be with Him (Luke 19:5–6). Zacchaeus needed Jesus, and so do we.

God knows you feel rejected and talked about and knows the enemy is trying to silence your praise. Keep praising the Lord over your critics. Keep serving even if they don't say thank you. Keep singing, keep praying, and keep going to work despite the hostile environment. Keep loving that sister or brother who despitefully misuses you. Keep praying for that wayward child, and forgive those who can't see past your weakness.

Yes, they talked about you. Yes, they laughed at you. And yes, they walked out on you. Allow the Lord to deal with them as He sees fit. Who knows, He may even choose to use you.

When we treat others with love, despite how we are treated, the assuredness of who we are in Christ becomes evident to them and to us.

I was broken after losing my first two babies before ever having the chance to hold them, and I was nearly crushed when certain people told me it was because of my sin. But in the midst of that pain, I was confident that since God allowed my miscarriages to take place, He must have a plan to see me through the grief. The closer I drew to the

Lord, the clearer His voice became. I had to see past the current state and see myself whole; I had to see myself the way God sees me. Then one day, I got a glimpse of who God called me to be and a glimpse was good enough for me.

If I had allowed the enemy to convince me that God was punishing me, I would have been stuck in a state of failure, never living or going after every one of God's promises for my life.

I had to experience God's faithfulness to me through many trials in order to come to a place where I realized how true this is. God also used this time to teach me that the world, my ministry, and my family are all watching how I treat people when they reject and accuse, and they're also watching how I respond to seasons of sorrow.

God has since blessed me with two amazing children who are still with me today. I need them to know their momma trusts in the Lord regardless of her current life situation.

The people in your life need to see that you trust in the Lord in the middle of seasons of suffering too. But more importantly, God sees how you respond to life's challenges, joys, and heartbreaks, and He longs for you to respond to them with trust in His unrelenting goodness. The more grace we receive from God in our times of need, the more equipped we are to extend grace to others.

WORKBOOK

Chapter Nine Questions

Question: What situations in your life leave you feeling defeated and doubting God's care? How have these situations been misjudged by others?

_____

_____

_____

_____

_____

_____

_____

_____

_____

_____

_____

Question: Describe a time when you categorized a person, only to later find out more of their story and understand their true hurts, value, and potential.

_____

_____

_____

_____

_____

_____

_____

_____

_____

_____

_____

_____

Action: What does God say about you? What does He call you? What are His labels for you? Looking through Scripture, start a list. Here are some verses to get started: Ephesians 1:3–14; John 15:15; Philippians 1:3–8.

Journal Prompt: Like Hannah did, pour out all your hurt to God and express your trust in His goodness and love for you.

Chapter Nine Notes

Forgiveness and Extending Grace

Therefore, as God's chosen people, holy and dearly loved,
clothe yourselves with compassion, kindness, humility,
gentleness and patience. Bear with each other and forgive
one another if any of you has a grievance against someone.
Forgive as the Lord forgave you. And over all these virtues
put on love, which binds them all together in perfect unity.
—*Colossians 3:12–14*

One of the hardest things I ever had to do was pray for someone who hurt me to my core. I was so hurt by her actions that I allowed it to send me on a downward spiral. I clearly remember hearing God tell me to pray for her, but I was so broken by what happened I couldn't pray.

Instead, I was overwhelmed with hurt, anger, and resentment to the point of obsession. I wanted to know why she behaved the way she had, and I went in search of my why. It was exhausting and endless, and I gained nothing but more pain. For months I thought about her and what she did to my family and to me. Then one morning after I had taken my daughter to school, I walked into my

bathroom and heard God's voice. He told me that if I continued down this road, the bitterness in my heart wouldn't
just destroy my life, it would also destroy our children's
lives.

I looked in the mirror and didn't like what I saw, and
immediately I called on Jesus. After I'd confessed all my
anger and hurt to Him, I began to pray for the woman who
had hurt me.

I have to admit, the first prayer for her was weak and
insincere. But every time the enemy brought the offense
to my mind, I started to pray. And each time I did, the
Holy Spirit revealed to me what I needed to pray for con-
cerning her. When I saw her needs, it allowed me to
extend grace. I don't know when it happened, but each
time I operated in forgiveness and grace, I felt freedom.
Twelve years have passed since then, and occasionally
when she comes to mind, I still feel the urge to pray for
her. The difference now is that when she comes to mind,
the offense doesn't consume me or cause me pain. It's
simply a reminder to pray for her.

Holding offenses is something all of us are good at.
Sometimes it's for little things like being cut off in traffic
or being treated rudely at the store. But some offenses are
life-altering: abandonment, abuse, theft, or even murder.
Such offenses leave behind wounds so deep we wonder if
we can ever be healed. How do you forgive someone who
has hurt you so deeply?

The first thing you do is remember that our ability to
forgive stems from the forgiveness we receive from God
through Christ's work on the cross.

We Forgive Because God Forgives

But God demonstrates his own love for us in this: While we were still sinners, Christ died for us.
—**Romans 5:8**

If anyone has a right to bear a grudge, it's God. As the Creator of the universe, He had every right to demand that justice be served the first time we sinned against Him. When Jesus went to the cross, He had not only been betrayed by Judas, but He was abandoned by nearly all of His followers.

And us? Sin was so much a part of our lives, we wouldn't have known to ask for God's forgiveness if He hadn't sent someone into our lives to tell us what sin was and why we needed to be forgiven.

Jesus gave us the greatest pardon ever. His mercy, grace, and compassion for sinners were shown to us *on the cross*. When Jesus entered into Jerusalem on the back of a colt, He knew what the outcome would be (Matthew 21:1–11). He knew the whole time when the people were shouting, "Hosanna! Hosanna, forever!" that a week later the same crowds would be shouting, "Crucify! Crucify!" (Matthew 27:22–23).

It had to be that way.

Jesus knew we needed grace and mercy, and, especially, redemption. Before He went to the grave for us, He did one last thing. He prayed. Not for vengeance against us, but for our forgiveness.

You see, grace is an essential part of God's character,

which explains why He is so loving and forgiving to us. God loves us and knows the truth about us. He knows we are imperfect and that we are going to wrong others and hold other's wrongs against them.

But He loves us despite that major failing. He knows the side of us that we want to keep hidden from others. He knows what is in our hearts, yet He still calls us His beloved.

The enemy, by contrast, is the one who wants you to hold on to the grief, the hurt, and the abuse. He is the one who continues to hit replay on that internal recorder in your mind. He doesn't care about you, and he doesn't care about the one who harmed you. He only cares that while you're angry and withholding forgiveness from those who've wronged you, you are withholding the fullness of God's blessing from your life.

Dear friend, we don't get a pass for unforgiveness because we are hurt. No one is without flaws or lives a sinless life. I know it hurts, and, yes, I get why you feel the way you do. But I also know God is offering healing and freedom to you now through His Son. But that healing can't begin as long as you continue to hold onto your grudges and hurts.

Why Must I Forgive?

There is no difference between Jew and Gentile, for all have sinned and fall short of the glory of God, and all are justified freely by his grace through the redemption that came by Christ Jesus.

—Romans 3:22b–24

As hard as it is to comprehend it at times, sin is sin. There is no difference. And believe it or not, unforgiveness is just as wrong in God's view as murder and theft. Why? Because when we refuse to forgive others, we designate ourselves as the judge. And that sets us in direct opposition to God. He alone has the authority to declare the verdict of guilty or not guilty.

Now that's not to say there should not be courts and legal systems or that lawbreakers should not face the consequences for their actions. That's another issue entirely.

God commanded that we forgive those who have wronged us just as He forgave us for sinning against Him (Matthew 6:14–15). But why do we have to forgive? It's important to remember forgiveness isn't about letting people off the hook for their actions. Instead, it allows God to step into situations and handle them as He best sees fit.

Forgiveness frees you as much as it frees the one who has sinned against you. It's like medicine for your soul. It sets free that which has been held up and what you have been holding on to and refusing to deal with. Unforgiveness tells God you don't trust His process and that you don't need His help. But forgiveness cuts through all that and tells God you surrendered your will to His will. Then God, without hesitation, will move in a miraculous way in your life.

Forgiveness removes avenues for Satan to operate in our lives. Jesus knew we would need to forgive others so that the enemy couldn't hold us hostage to our hurt and grief. Forgiveness frees God to work in the hearts and lives of those who sin against us, even if we never see them again.

Forgiveness protects you in your ministry to others. It enables you to see into the brokenness of others so that you can come alongside them on their healing journeys. It checks your motives when you speak out against sins within the body of Christ. And it prevents you from falling into a similar sin as the person who sinned against you—even if that person sinned against you multiple times.

How Often Must I Forgive?

Then Peter came up and said to him, "Lord, how often will my brother sin against me, and I forgive him? As many as seven times?" Jesus said to him, "I do not say to you seven times, but seventy-seven times."
—***Matthew 18:21–22*** *(ESV)*

It's hard to forgive someone who continually does the same thing over and over again—especially when there seems to be no concern for the resulting hurt. Surely there must be a limit on how many times we forgive.

Hotheaded Peter asked that very question after Jesus told a parable about forgiveness. Jesus' response? Continue to forgive them just as the Father continues to forgive you.

Forgiveness is about extending grace even when we least feel like giving it, including if it's a habitual sin that a fellow believer is truly struggling to overcome. Like it or not, we all have things in our lives we constantly have to apologize for—particularly where our words are concerned.

When we continue to extend mercy and forgiveness to other believers who can't seem to stop making the same mistakes over and over, it reminds them that they have a Father who cares for them and wants to see them set free of whatever is holding them captive. Our forgiveness also encourages them in the midst of an enemy that wants to cause them additional sorrow and harm the entire body of Christ (2 Corinthians 2:5–11).

Forgiveness Restores

True forgiveness in the life of the believer heals and restores life to the body and soul. It reunites us with our Father and guards us from the enemy. When we allow God's forgiveness to work its way in and through us, it reveals to the world that the God we follow isn't a God who delights in condemning us for our wrongs or who waits to strike us down. Instead, ours is a God who delights in restoring the bruised, the broken, and the lost. True forgiveness allows us to experience and show God's grace. And we must be equipped with these skills as we serve God in whatever ministry He has called us.

WORKBOOK

Chapter Ten Questions

Question: Describe a time when someone harmed or offended you and you allowed unforgiveness to poison your life. How did your bitter spirit affect others around you? How did it damage your walk with God?

_____

_____

_____

_____

_____

_____

_____

_____

_____

_____

Question: Describe a time that you received forgiveness. How did receiving grace from another help reveal to you the nature of God's grace and forgiveness toward you?

_____

_____

_____

_____

_____

_____

_____

_____

_____

_____

_____

Action: Make a list of what forgiveness is and what it is not. If there is someone in your life that you are struggling to forgive, make a commitment to pray for that person daily.

Journal Prompt: Make a list of some of the things that God has forgiven you for and the sins/bondage from which He has set you free. Then above or below your list write "Forgive as the Lord forgave you." Write out your commitment to choose forgiveness over bitterness when you are hurt by others.

Chapter Ten Notes

CHAPTER ELEVEN

Growth and Maturity

Now there are varieties of gifts, but the same Spirit; and there are varieties of service, but the same Lord; and there are varieties of activities, but it is the same God who empowers them all in everyone.
—*1 Corinthians 12:4–6* *(ESV)*

Have you ever known people who are restless where they are in life? Friends, family members, or coworkers? Maybe you heard them say they should be doing more, or perhaps they change careers often and question why God hasn't answered their prayers yet?

Perhaps you've felt this way at some point in time. You're just ready to move to the next stage of life. You feel like you're not accomplishing anything, but everyone around you seems to be progressing at a faster pace. You can't figure out what the problem is—surely your level of expertise should be used to make a bigger impact. But instead you feel stuck training others and not getting the promotion or singing in the choir but not leading the solo.

If truth be told, maybe you're even struggling with feelings of jealousy because someone you know is further along in ministry than you. We live in a society that measures value and worth based on external appearances. Unfortunately this same belief has infiltrated the church. We judge a ministry based on the number of people attending, on how far our platform reaches, and how much money we're raising to *do God's work*.

This is especially dangerous when young believers become discouraged because they feel they're ready to jump into the next stage of their ministry before they have the actual growth and maturity needed to step into such a place of authority. I believe part of this is because of our obsession with celebrity. We want to be seen to be known and to have a sense of worth.

The truth is God did not call us to be celebrities. He called us to serve and love one another, which doesn't necessarily require a platform. If that is where God has placed you, certainly His will shall be done, however be sure God has done the placing. He may have placed you in a small community or church for His purpose. Trust the process. All of the steps are necessary, so don't bypass any of the steps. God knows where you are and the reason you're headed in that direction.

Spiritual Maturity

And I, brethren, could not speak to you as to spiritual men, but as to men of flesh, as to infants in Christ. I gave you milk to drink, not solid food; for you were not yet able to receive it. Indeed, even now you are not yet able, for you are still fleshly. For since there is jealousy and strife among

you, are you not fleshly, and are you not walking like mere men?
—1 Corinthians 3:1–4 *(NASB)*

Growth and spiritual maturity come when we learn to forgive offenses, when we serve without having our names called, and when we realize our *platform is portable*. It is wherever God sends us. We miss the mark when we overlook those standing in front of us who are in need of Jesus because we're more focused on how we want to be perceived than on whom we are called to serve.

Your platform is in your home, on the job, and in the marketplace. But we are too busy looking for a crowd. Besides, God knows exactly who He can use as well as where and what gifts and talents to give to them. The fact that you don't have a traveling ministry or a megachurch platform won't limit you from giving God your best where you are and reaching those He wants you to reach.

That's the point I tried to convey to one individual with whom I was working. The more I interacted with him, the more I realized his longing to be seen and heard came from a place of brokenness. There were things in his life—hurts he hadn't faced and problems he hadn't dealt with—that would need to be addressed between him and God before he was ready to be placed into a position of authority. Let's take a look at how one person from the Bible dealt with hurts and brokenness before being used by God.

Joseph's Tale: A Story of Maturing Faith

And we know that for those who love God all things work

together for good, for those who are called according to his purpose.
—Romans 8:28 *(ESV)*

One day while in prayer, I was reminded by the Holy Spirit of the biblical account of Joseph and the difficulties he had gone through before God fulfilled the dream He placed in Joseph's life (Genesis 37–50).

Joseph had to be matured for God to use him to bless a nation. Joseph learned temperance through rejection and loss. First, he was betrayed by his brothers and sold into slavery, then he was accused of a crime he didn't commit, then he was forgotten about after being promised that his case would be brought before Pharaoh. But through each hardship, Joseph grew in maturity and wisdom. He chose to reject bitterness and learned to see God's bigger picture. And when the time came, God fulfilled the promise He'd made to Joseph as a child.

We all go through things in life that challenge our faith, our worth, and our sense of self. Whether it's our health, careers, relationships, or struggles that leave us questioning "why?" It's not until we begin to heal from those wounds that we can honestly say, "What the Enemy meant for evil, God used for good" (Genesis 50:20).

Never forget that God knows where you are at all times. He knows what you're capable of and what He is able to accomplish through you. But He will not move you into what He has for you next until you've completed the work that needs to be done where you are now—both in your life and the lives of others.

So if you feel like you're on the sideline, don't stop

practicing and cheering for your team. When you're at work, don't envy someone else's success; keep supporting the mission. Your time will come, but you have to be ready. By the time Joseph's dream was manifested, he was a changed man; he did not hold bitterness in his heart. He was able to see God's plan for his life, understanding that all that happened had to happen. In short, he had reached a maturity in the Lord.

Maturing in Wisdom and Grace

But as for you, you meant evil against me; but God meant it for good, in order to bring it about as it is this day, to save many people alive.
—Genesis 50:20 *(NKJV)*

We can definitely agree that Joseph was hurt by the things he experienced in life. But what if Joseph couldn't get past what his brothers did? What if he had never used the gift God had given him to interpret the cupbearer's dream? How long would he have been in prison? How long would he have delayed his future because he was offended and hurt?

How we respond to offenses directs the way we act. It's almost like you have to pause in the moments of trouble and ask yourself, "Will I take an optimistic approach, learn from it, and keep moving forward, or will I lash out and stew in it until I've made my point?"

Asking those questions before you react, helps to determine the best outcome for all parties concerned. Spiritual growth and maturity draw you to the heart of

God, not away from Him, and it certainly doesn't leave us sitting in the center of offenses.

There are times we have been or will be wounded or offended by those who have been called to protect us, love us, and lead us, but who have done so without wisdom and love for God's people. Indeed, it seems the climate and attitude of the believers in some churches have become insensitive to the needs of people who are in search of acceptance and love. But we can change that by being aware of how we love and how we serve, especially when we have been mistreated like Joseph.

Emotional wounds are among the most common reasons people are hindered in their spiritual growth. We cannot be all that God desires for us to be or experience the fullness of joy and abundant living if we don't address the emotional wounds that we'd like to remain hidden and which cause us to respond to adult situations with infant-like responses.

Sometimes our spiritual growth is held up because a spiritual war is being waged and we didn't even know it. Instead we fight the wrong battles and often with the wrong weapons.

Never forget, you are in a war that wants to remain hidden so that you remain wounded. This war wounds its victims within the heart and mind causing injury that surfaces as physical and mental abuse, rejection, fear, isolations, insecurity, depression, and shame. When we change our mindset and understand who is behind those negative emotions and behavior, we can change how we react and respond.

Sometimes maturity comes in recognizing that you

need help and reaching out for it. If you are struggling with something that requires godly, professional help to move past, don't hesitate to get assistance. What you learn through the experience may very well be the tools you need to step into a future ministry God is even now preparing for you. Your healing is part of what God is doing in your life.

Your Testimony Matters

No one has the same testimony you have. You are a living witness of God's mercy, His grace, and even His miracles. There are things in your life that God has done for you that no one else could have done.

This current generation needs you. They need wise men and women speaking into their lives and showing them what right looks like, just like you had someone come and help you at some point in your life. Chances are that you are that person who God will use to help strengthen their walk of faith and introduce them to Jesus. They need men and women who will not compromise the truth of God's word to fit in with what feels good but leaves their spirit empty.

God may not need you to set foot on a stage to speak to one hundred thousand people. He may only need you to speak into the life of one.

Never doubt the importance of that simple act of obedience. There's no such thing as a small ministry or a big ministry in God's plan. There's only His ministry to seek out and save the lost and wounded—wherever they may be.

Recognizing that God uses you according to His will and timing is part of the process of reaching spiritual maturity. There is a spiritual war for your soul so this maturity will not come easily, but God has provided you with everything you need to live victoriously.

Chapter Eleven Questions

Question: How would you describe your current platform for ministry in comparison to your dream platform? What is God accomplishing with you in the place where you currently are? Are you content and growing as you serve where He has placed you—why or why not?

_____

_____

_____

_____

_____

_____

_____

_____

_____

_____

_____

_____

Question: Can a person have a large ministry without a true anointing for it? Why or why not? What are some of the dangers of a person having celebrity status before being spiritually mature and ready for that sort of platform?

_____

_____

_____

_____

_____

_____

_____

_____

_____

_____

_____

Action: Read a biography of someone whom you consider a giant in the faith. How did this person serve in unseen and unglamorous ways? Was their celebrity status something that they strove to achieve or that resulted from a life of extraordinary commitment and obedience to God? How do you know?

Journal Prompt: Thank God for the opportunities for ministry He has placed before you right now. Then evaluate each one and consider if you are making the most of that opportunity. What areas of woundedness and immaturity do you need to work through in your life so that God can use you more completely?

Chapter Eleven Notes

CHAPTER TWELVE

Discernment and Leadership

*Let us not become weary in doing good, for at the proper
time we will reap a harvest if we do not give up. Therefore,
as we have opportunity, let us do good to all people, especially to those who belong to the family of believers.*
—Galatians 6:9–10

Have you ever experienced a time in your life when no
matter what you did to avoid trouble it just seemed to
show up anyway? You try to do what you know to be
right, going through life minding your business, and the
enemy sends trouble your way?

When you're a child of God operating in the spirit of
peace and obedience, you're going to come up against
some opposition that will challenge what you know to be
right. Do not be fooled. Satan will actively work to sabotage your sense of peace when you're trying to honor God.
Unfortunately he often uses the people in our lives to carry
the ammunition and that can include members of your
family and the church.

The Apostle Paul was no stranger to this tactic. In fact he wrote his letter to the Galatians for this very reason. Here was a group of Christians who had a passion and zeal for their faith, but along came a group of other believers with a list of rules and regulations that no one, not even the rule bringers, could live up to (Galatians 6:12–15). And it was causing the Galatians to flounder in their faith.

Why does Satan do this? Because the more distracted we are by doubts, insecurities, and conflicts in our private lives and public ministries, the more we're unable to effectively shine the light of the gospel into the spiritual darkness that oppresses our homes and communities. Make no mistake, Satan wants you to fail. He can't possess you, but he can influence you and those around you. But when you are able to identify the spirits he's sending into your life, you'll be able to recognize them for what they are and reject them from your life.

I will tell you briefly about one particular spirit that may come against you in your ministry. It is devious and deadly and nearly took me out of ministry altogether.

While meeting with a godly woman I deeply respect, I shared some difficulties I'd been encountering within my spirit as I ministered alongside certain people.

She immediately cried out, "Oh baby, that is a Jezebel spirit!" Wow! I had heard about it, heard pastors preach on it, and maybe even experienced it in my youth, but not like this. I had to truly understand what the spirit was before I could deal with it properly.

The Jezebel Spirit

There was never anyone like Ahab, who sold himself to do evil in the eyes of the LORD, urged on by Jezebel his wife.
—1 Kings 21:25

Jezebel was the wicked, sinful wife of King Ahab of Israel during the time of Elijah. She was also a priestess of the false god Baal. During this time, Israel turned completely away from God and completely gave itself over to the worship of Baal.

Jezebel was so powerful that even Elijah, the prophet of the Lord who called down fire from heaven, ran in fear when she threatened his life (1 Kings 19:2–3). She was so wicked that when King Ahab was refused the sale of a nearby vineyard, Jezebel ordered the leaders of his town to declare a feast and have two men accuse the man of blaspheming against God and the king and then to put him to death. She was powerful enough that the leaders of the town did as they were told without question, and an innocent man was murdered (1 Kings 21).

Jezebel was a woman who had completely given herself over to her god, who was nothing more than an evil spirit. And that evil spirit led her to her destruction (2 Kings 9:30–37).

Identifying a Jezebel Spirit

But there were also false prophets among the people, just as there will be false teachers among you. They will secretly introduce destructive heresies, even denying the

sovereign Lord who bought them—bringing swift destruc-
tion on themselves.

—2 Peter 2:1

A Jezebel spirit is a demonic spirit that ultimately seeks to control and rule over people, especially God's people and a prophetic ministry. This spirit needs to be seen. It takes on the strongest character trait of the individual it is using.

If an individual is envious of others, then you'll see that person operating in jealousy under the influence of a Jezebel spirit. If the tactic is bullying, intimidation is the weapon used and the targets are generally those who are seemingly meek and mild-mannered. If the spirit is not allowed to lead, it will go out of its way to sabotage the growth of an organization and the forward movement of those who want to serve.

Individuals influenced by a Jezebel spirit need to be elevated above everyone else. They'll find a way to demean your success by using disparaging remarks. They boast about what a powerful anointing they have and demand that everyone around them affirm them in this. They don't know how to highlight others, but rather they need the spotlight on themselves. But they also know the right words to say and things to do in order to convince others in the church or ministry that they are genuine.

Identifying a Jezebel spirit is only the beginning. Defending against such a spirit is critical, and God's Word gives us vital instruction.

Defending Against a Jezebel Spirit

But the fruit of the Spirit is love, joy, peace, forbearance, kindness, goodness, faithfulness, gentleness and self-control. Against such things there is no law.
—Galatians 5:22–23

We have to be careful that babes in the faith are not attached to those under the influence of a Jezebel spirit because they will grow up deformed and malnourished, lacking spiritual maturity, growth, and power. Like their leaders, such believers will have a form of godliness but not holiness. As you grow in your spiritual maturity and step into roles of leadership, it is important that you use wisdom when assigning responsibility to those who have just come to Christ and when deciding whom to align them with for mentorship. When evaluating those in leadership, ask God to reveal if their words and actions are holy and right. As you spend time in the Word and prayer, you'll be able to identify who is being directed by the Holy Spirit and who is not.

The genuine traits of the Holy Spirit are evident in the lives of the men and women truly seeking after God and serving with a servant's heart. These people build up and encourage those they come into contact with. They bring unity into areas rife with strife. They are kind and compassionate without seeking favors in return. And above all, they preach the gospel of Christ alone.

I learned to shore myself up against a Jezebel spirit— as well as any potential accusations of impropriety— while training for a security job in which I worked with sensitive information in a secure location. I learned that I had to be aware of the tactics the adversary uses to gain information that could weaken the infrastructure of an organization. Some activities and techniques used by the adversary may be quite sophisticated, and we might be targeted without even realizing it.

Isn't that exactly what Satan does? He targets you from the moment you were born, and he does not stop until your life here ceases.

Now if a corporation practices good protocol for securing its infrastructure, why aren't we more vigilant of imminent attacks launched against us? Security officials warn that you should be aware of certain suspicious behaviors when traveling to foreign countries. Well, what would happen if we incorporated the same watchful attitude for spiritual attacks?

Below are suggestions for personal security when traveling abroad, with my interpretations of spiritual applications no matter where you are.[8]

Limit or eliminate talking about sensitive information. It's not necessary to share every detail of your life or testimony with everyone around you.

Keep items of value with you and never leave them unattended. Cover your family, your children, and loved ones with prayer, and be mindful of who you spend your time with.

Ignore or deflect intrusive inquiries or conversation about business and personal matters. Pay attention to the urging of the Holy Spirit when you're conversing with others. Chances are, if it doesn't feel right, it probably isn't right. Seek God through prayer and fasting until He reveals the truth of the situation.

Avoid situations that could be used for future exploitation against you. Conduct yourself today in a manner that represents God. Turn from dangerous or tempting situations and repent your sin so when the accuser of the brethren comes, Jesus tells the Father that He already paid for that.

Maintain a low profile—blend into your surroundings. Surround yourself with people who will pray with you and encourage you; do not be conformed to this world but be renewed by studying the Word of God (Romans 12:2).

Report anything unusual or suspicious—see something, say something. Be sharp and use discernment. Just because people are in leadership doesn't automatically mean they are godly individuals.

How interesting it is to see that we will protect our personal items and surroundings but not give the same attention to our spiritual awareness and safety. Don't compromise your spiritual security: we have to be keenly aware of the counterintelligence that takes place in the realm of spiritual warfare. I continue to be made aware of how Jezebel shifts and changes shape, appearance, and position. But we must continue to seek the heart of God and trust the guidance of the Holy Spirit, which sheds light on who we are really dealing with.

I don't get mad. Instead, I get ready and position my-self for battle, putting on the full armor of God from Ephesians 6:13–17. It's never easy, but I have the assur-ance that God is always with me—and God wants to be with you, too. He wants you to be keenly aware of what and whom you are dealing with and to have the right tools to take into battle.

Whom Are We Fighting?

Many will follow their depraved conduct and will bring the way of truth into disrepute. In their greed these teachers will exploit you with fabricated stories. Their condemnation has long been hanging over them, and their destruction has not been sleeping.
—2 Peter 2:2–3

A Jezebel spirit takes its cues from the father of lies, Satan himself (John 8:44). He uses fear, envy, and divi-sion to keep the people of God in bondage and spiritual blindness. This Jezebel spirit goes around to seek out those with similar motives and similar strengths. It re-cruits the weak or less informed and those operating out of rebellion because they are more pliable. It looks for fa-miliar spirits and develops close-knit cliques.

This spirit tends to move from one church to the next, campaigning and lobbying for those with whom they can form an alliance. Scripture tells us in the Book of Ezekiel how Lucifer alienated the loyalty of the angels he was given charge over:

You were perfect in your ways from the day you were created, till iniquity was found in you. By the abundance of your trading you became filled with violence within, and you sinned...

—Ezekiel 28:15–16a *(NKJV)*

It should come as no surprise that once this Jezebel spirit is exposed, it will do all it can to accuse and bring enmity between you and those you are trying to serve and love. This is a spirit that requires you to be fully covered by the Holy Spirit when you go up against it. This is not a battle you can win on your own.

When you seek the Holy Spirit in situations where you suspect a Jezebel spirit is at work, He will open your eyes to the truth of the situation. And if He directs you to speak out against it, He'll give you the strength and words to do so. Your actions may not be popular or even welcomed. You may find yourself being chased out of your church or ministry. Don't let that prevent you from obeying what God has asked you to do.

God is a loving and patient Father, but there is a limit to His patience. He will not tolerate the Jezebel spirit in His church, and He'll bring to light all who have aligned themselves with it. Be careful that you are not one of them.

We will encounter Jezebel spirits. The enemy is comfortable with you trying to fight them on your own, but once you call on the name of Jesus, he knows he is defeated. You have to continue to seek God, spend time in

His word, pray, and fast so you are armed with the weapons of spiritual warfare. Guarding against a Jezebel spirit will ensure that you can be effective ministering to others. As a Christian—and especially one in ministry—the spiritual warfare you will experience will extend beyond a Jezebel spirit. Read on to be further equipped against the schemes of Satan.

Chapter Twelve Questions

Question: When and how have you encountered a *Jezebel spirit* at work in your church or ministry? How did this spirit display itself as having *a form of godliness but not holiness*?

_____

_____

_____

_____

_____

_____

_____

_____

_____

_____

Question: How should a mature believer respond when someone comes to them trying to stir up division? What is the difference between spreading gossip and sharing truth? How and in what manner should sin be exposed, particularly sin within the leadership of a ministry?

_____

_____

_____

_____

_____

_____

_____

_____

_____

_____

_____

Action: Make a list of the sort of people that Jesus and the apostles warned the early Christians to look out for. Give examples of how these sorts of people operate in the church today. Scriptures to start your search: Matthew 7:15; Luke 12:1, 15; Luke 20:45–47; Romans 16:17; 3 John 9–10.

Journal Prompt: If there is someone in your ministry who is causing division, striving for control, or demanding the spotlight, spend time in prayer asking God for discernment about the underlying issues going on and how you should respond to this person. Commit to following His leading and to steering clear of a Jezebel spirit yourself.

Chapter Twelve Notes

CHAPTER THIRTEEN

Spiritual Warfare

Be alert and of sober mind. Your enemy the devil prowls around like a roaring lion looking for someone to devour.
—1 Peter 5:8

Have you ever looked around on a clear day and admired how the blue sky stretched on for miles? Have you ever wondered what makes up the atmosphere? Perhaps you're a scientist or science enthusiast who is able to fully explain the mix and breakdown of oxygen and other gases that fill the air around us enabling life to exist on our planet. Sadly, that's not me. The best way I know to explain the atmosphere is that it has a layer of gases surrounding the earth, held in place by gravity.

In the simplest of terms, I suppose one could say the atmosphere is a semi-invisible border that surrounds the earth and protects it from the vacuum of space. Interestingly, the word *air* is sometimes used interchangeably with *atmosphere* to represent the emotional charge of a room, such as "the air or the atmosphere was thick with tension."

In both cases, atmosphere is something that is present, but not necessarily visible to the human eye. It has strength and power to it, sometimes beyond what we give it credit for. The same is true of spiritual forces.

With few exceptions, humanity is generally blind to angelic and demonic forces—at least with our physical eyes. There are those who are sensitive enough to sense the presence of a spirit in a room, and there are numerous cases where God has sent messages to individuals through His angels.

We discussed numerous times in the course of this book about the enemy who roams around the earth bent on our destruction. We've touched on the war being raged around us by Satan and his fallen angels. Even though we rarely see his army, we see the effects their attacks have on our world, just as we see the effects of the atmosphere holding in life and keeping out death.

The Fallen Archangel

In order to stand against an enemy, it's important to know who that enemy is. Satan was a mighty angel, the archangel who was responsible for setting the atmosphere of worship in heaven. He had access to God and was in charge of many other angels (Ezekiel 28:12–14).

Satan, who was called Lucifer, was cast out of heaven because he wanted to be equal with God. He desired to have power, he wanted to be worshipped, and he wanted the throne. So he persuaded a third of the angels to rise up against God and rebel. Satan was consumed by egotism and was cast out from heaven because of his pride and rebellion (Isaiah 14:12–15).

And then God created us, man and woman, in His image (Genesis 1:27). Why does Satan hate us? He witnessed God's love for man up close when God stepped down from heaven and gave us the very best part of Him. He saw how God place so much love and care into creating an atmosphere for man in the Garden of Eden. God placed His face on man's face and breathed life into him. We are the *Imago Dei*—the image of God. And since he hates God, he hates the image of God and he wants to see everything that God created destroyed.

Satan loves to deceive believers and nonbelievers into thinking he doesn't exist or that he's not quite as bad as we've been led to think, especially in a feel-good society that says it doesn't believe in that "Jesus stuff."

The truth is Satan exists and he is very much a threat to us. In fact, Satan is called the "the prince of the power of the air" (Ephesians 2:2 ESV). Just as we can't see or touch the air but we know it is there, the same is true of the devil.

Satan may be a prince of sorts, and, like a human prince, he possesses power. The Greek term for prince in Ephesians 2:2, *archon*, indicates a person endowed with power, but not necessarily by birth.[7] Satan didn't inherit authority—he exercises authority through persuasive force.

But Jesus is the royal heir. He is the Prince of Peace who reigns in power because of His father in heaven. God does not need to introduce a thought to persuade us; it is not God's nature to control us or to be cunning and deceptive. He has given us free will to choose all things, and He coaxes us with love and grace.

1 John tells us that the world is currently controlled by Satan, the evil one. John also tells us in his epistle that Satan is directly opposed to the life Christ brings, as Satan only wants to steal, kill, and destroy those whom Christ seeks to redeem. Having control of the world, he takes advantage of natural human tendencies—such as envy, anger, rage, and lust—to derail followers of God. In particular, if Satan can convince you to see yourself or others from a viewpoint at odds with God's truth, then he can persuade you to act on those misguided convictions.

The way we think or perceive something determines how we operate in that area. If we see something as fun and not requiring too much work, we might jump right in, even if that thing is harmful. But if it seems out of reach, challenging, or a bit uncomfortable, we might avoid it at all cost, even if it is beneficial and the direction in which God is calling us.

I believe the mind is where spiritual warfare begins, which is why Scripture calls us to take control of our thoughts (2 Corinthians 10:4–5).

Arrest Your Thoughts

Since Satan is a spirit, he does not have a body. His interactions with the physical realm are limited, therefore, he searches to see whom he can manipulate and destroy. His actions today are no different than in the garden when he first approached Eve. He planted a seed of doubt into her mind that led her to pick the fruit and eat it herself.

He is still hard at work planting those deadly seeds. Any thought that is self-defeating, loathsome, wicked, and does not honor God is specifically designed by the enemy to take hold of your mind and make you a prisoner to sin.

Just as he did with Eve, Satan introduces negative and deceptive thoughts with the intent to destroy your knowledge and understanding of God. If he can destroy what you see and your ability to understand truth, he can cause you to forget that you were made in God's image. He can't separate Christians from the Father, but he can take you out of the fight.

You must take authority over the air because if you don't you will be besieged with thoughts that draw you away from the knowledge of God—thoughts that are negative and, for many, result in anxiety and depression. You have to take authority of your thoughts, or arrest your thoughts, and command your mind in Jesus name to become subject to the will and knowledge of who God is. This is how we "[cast] down arguments and every high thing that exalts itself against the knowledge of God" (2 Corinthians 10:5 NKJV).

So why is Satan so intent on destroying humanity? Well, one reason is that he already knows he is defeated and wants to keep as many people from God as possible. He wants to keep us disillusioned and distant from God. He hates man and is jealous of God's love for us.

Spiritual Warfare

The apostle Paul cautions us to "stand against the devil's schemes" and describes spiritual armor that helps defend believers against the acts of terror and hatred Satan unleashes on God's children (Ephesians 6:10–20).

> *For we do not wrestle against flesh and blood, but against principalities, against powers, against the rulers of the darkness of this age, against spiritual hosts of wickedness in the heavenly places.*
> **—Ephesians 6:12** *(NKJV)*

Paul clearly tells us who we are fighting against. He tells us to guard ourselves against everything that tries to elevate itself against the knowledge of God (2 Corinthians 10:4–5). Christians often call this spiritual warfare.

Too often we respond to a situation based on who has hurt us or what has come against us, seeing only what is in the natural. We don't automatically think there is something working against us behind the scenes. But that's what the enemy wants us to think. He wants to remain hidden so that you continue to fight against the wrong thing.

In his letter to the scattered church, Peter warned his brothers and sisters in Christ to be alert and focused so that they could clearly see the enemy's attacks and stand against them (1 Peter 5:8–9). He also told them to take courage that they were not alone in this battle (1 Peter 5:10).

Stand Firm

> *Stand firm then, with the belt of truth buckled around your*

*waist, with the breastplate of righteousness in place, and
with your feet fitted with the readiness that comes from
the gospel of peace.*
                                            —Ephesians 6:14–15

It's interesting that we fight in a realm we can't see,
but we feel every blow, every jab, and every piercing of
the enemy's arrow. It can be wearying and disheartening.
God is so merciful and He does not leave us defenseless
(Psalm 116:6). He watches over us (1 Peter 3:12). He protects and covers us (Psalm 91:4–6). And He goes before
us in battle (Deuteronomy 1:30). He also gives us the
weapons and armor to stand firm against the "fiery darts
of the wicked one" (Ephesians 6:16 NKJV).

One of our chief weapons is prayer. When we pray, our
faith is activated in our heart and mind—an invisible
realm—and we are strengthened in the Lord's power.
Alone we are no match for the enemy, but our heavenly
Father has given us everything we need to withstand the
devil through prayer and fasting. One form of prayer that
we can take up is fasting. When we fast as a sign of sacrifice and obedience, we are telling God we choose Him
over distractions, no matter what they might be. Fasting
can clear our mind and allow us to hear more clearly from
Him.

Our other weapon is the Word of God. When we take
the time to study Scripture on our own rather than depending on others to tell us what they think it says, we are
better able to recognize thoughts and suggestions that do
not line up with the Word. When we do this, we can arrest
the atmosphere and bring every thought under the

authority of the Word of God (2 Corinthians 10:4–5).

If you find yourself falling prey to Satan's attacks, just remember that nothing can separate you from the love of God (Romans 8:38–39). Jesus came to call the backslider back to Him and to draw us back into an active and whole relationship with the Father. Jesus is calling those who have fallen, have failures, and think they can't be used by God. One of the many lies the enemy uses to fill your head with is that God won't use you or accept you because of your past. Dear friend, that is the greatest lie of all.

I have to admit, certain times are especially challenging because it feels so much easier to remain complacent in our sin. During those times, I have to be honest with myself and say, *"Demi, you are going to mess this up. Why are you putting yourself through this?"* And that's when I pray, *"Lord, I can't, but You can."* I might have to say it more than once to finally reach the place where I believe what I'm saying, but the moment I ask God to enter into a situation—be it an emotional struggle, a physical confrontation, or an obstacle preventing me from moving forward in my life—God steps in with His strength and His peace.

This is evident in the book of Daniel. Chapter 10 tells us that the messenger of the Lord, an angel, had been in battle with an evil spirit—"the prince of the Persian kingdom"—so he could explain Daniel's most recent vision to him (Daniel 10:13–14). In verse 12, the messenger angel told Daniel, who had been fasting, that God had heard him from the moment he had set his heart to understand and humble himself before God. The angel explicitly stated that he had come in response to Daniel's *words*—the words he had spoken to God in faith and humility.

Dear friend, when God stands with you, Satan can't stand against you (James 4:7). He may rage, he may press, and he may try to threaten and confuse you or even come against you physically through illness or loss. But you must remember, he's fighting a losing battle. Call on your identity as a child of God and resist the devil. He will have no choice but to flee from you (James 4:7). In doing so, you change the atmosphere around you and, ultimately, your life.

WORKBOOK

Chapter Thirteen Questions

Question: What evidences of a constantly raging spiritual warfare do you see in the culture around you? What about in your own life?

_____

_____

_____

_____

_____

_____

_____

_____

_____

_____

_____

Question: Just as he did with Eve, Satan introduces negative and deceptive thoughts with the intent to destroy your knowledge and understanding of God. What are some of the negative or deceptive thoughts Satan commonly uses against you, and how do these lies destroy your knowledge and understanding of God?

For example, Satan may introduce the lie that a person's worth is measured by physical appearance and skill. Those believing that lie may become angry with God for the way He made them, or they may refuse to believe He is their Creator and instead decide they are an "accident."

_____

_____

_____

_____

_____

_____

_____

_____

_____

_____

_____

Action: Study and memorize Ephesians 6:10–18, which details the spiritual armor of believers. How can each part of this armor prepare and protect you for spiritual warfare?

Journal Prompt: Spend time in prayer asking God to reveal to you the areas where you are most vulnerable to spiritual warfare. What thoughts is Satan trying to plant in your mind? What Scriptures can you use to refute those lies?

Chapter Thirteen Notes

_____

_____

_____

_____

_____

_____

_____

_____

_____

_____

_____

_____

_____

_____

_____

_____

_____

_____

_____

_____

_____

_____

CONCLUSION

God Came for You

Many of the Samaritans from that town believed in him be-
cause of the woman's testimony, "He told me everything I
ever did." So when the Samaritans came to him, they urged
him to stay with them, and he stayed two days. And be-
cause of his words many more became believers.
—John 4:39–41

In the introduction to this book, I shared the story of
the woman at the well (John 4:1–26). She was a woman
living in sin and a member of a people shunned by the
people of Israel. And still, Jesus went out of His way to
speak specifically to her. Her testimony in turn led to the
salvation of many more.

This is the beautiful story of God's redemption. This is
your story.

The God who created the universe is the same God who
created you. He sees you. He knows where you are. He
knows what you're going through. He knows all the lies,
all the mistakes, all the hurts. And He has moved heaven
and hell to meet you right where you are.

Your life is a testimony of God's mercy. Your relationship with Him not only models how you will experience each relationship in your life, but also impacts how you share the gospel. My prayer is that you'll be like the Samaritan woman at the well who ran back to her town to tell anyone she met to come and meet the One who knew everything about her and covered her with His mercy, His compassion, and His healing grace.

REFERENCES

Notes

1. Miles, Austin. "In the Garden." 1913. *Hymnary.org.* https://hymnary.org/text/i_come_to_the_garden_alon e.

2. Keller, Phillip. *A Shepherd Looks at Psalm 23.* Zondervan, 1981, p. 114–115.

3. Spafford, Horatio, and Philip Bliss. "It Is Well." 1873. *Hymnary.org.* https://hymnary.org/text/when_peace_ like_a_river_attendeth_my_way.

4. Spafford and Bliss, "It Is Well."

5. Reagan, David. "The Threshingfloor." *LearntheBible.org.* http://www.learnthebible.org/the-threshingfloor.html.

6. Brown, Francis, Samuel Rolles Driver, and Charles Augustus Briggs. *Enhanced Brown-Driver-Briggs Hebrew and English Lexicon.* Clarendon Press, 1977, p. 712.

7. Strong, James. "G758 – archon." *Strong's Exhaustive*

Concordance of the Bible. Hunt & Eaton, 1894. In *Blue Letter Bible.* https://www.blueletterbible.org/lang/lexicon/lexicon.cfm?Strongs=G758&t=KJV.

8. "2018 Security Reindoctrination Desk Reference." *SAIC.* https://www.saic.com/sites/default/files/2018-11/Security-reindoc-2018-final.pdf.

9. Strong, James. "H7402 – rakal.*" Strong's Exhaustive Concordance of the Bible.* Hunt & Eaton, 1894. In *Blue Letter Bible.* https://www.blueletterbible.org/lang/lexicon/lexicon.cfm?t=kjv&strongs=h7402.

About the Author

Born and raised in Mississippi, Demi Thompson is a proud military spouse who retired with her husband to Northern Virginia after living in three countries and seven states. She is an alumnus of Liberty University, with graduate degrees in human services and in marriage and family counseling. Passionate about worship and intercession, Demi also manages to find time for baking, journaling, and trying out new Pinterest projects. She has been married to Ernest for twenty-six years, and they have two children, Sydney and Kyle.

Demi has personally seen lives changed and hearts healed as a result of her witness in sharing excerpts from her devotional time with God. She believes in the power of the same gospel that has healed her heart to heal the wounded and broken hearts of countless others.

Her prayer is that the simple knowledge in this book will be a resource and a tool to help bring people throughout the world to Christ—people who may be hurting but who desire to know Him and know who they are in Him.

73659179R00096

Made in the
USA
Middletown, DE